C**MORE**
Canada
firsts

MORE
Canada
firsts

DUFF CONACHER

Canadian Cataloguing in Publication Data

Conacher, Duff
    More Canada firsts : another collection of Canadian firsts and foremosts in the world

Includes bibliographical references.
ISBN 0-7710-2244-1

1. Canada – Civilization – Miscellanea.   2. World records – Canada.
I. Title.

FC95.C66 1999   971   C99-932481-0
F1021.C64 1999

We acknowledge the financial support of the Government of Canada through the Book Publishing Industry Development Program for our publishing activities. Canadä

We further acknowledge the support of the Canada Council for the Arts and the Ontario Arts Council for our publishing program.

Printed and bound in Canada

McClelland & Stewart Inc.
The Canadian Publishers
481 University Avenue
Toronto, Ontario
M5G 2E9

1 2 3 4 5   03 02 01 00 99

CONTENTS

ARTS

FOREWORD

This new collection by Duff Conacher of Canadian firsts and fore-mosts in the world extends our 1992 book *Canada Firsts* in terms of the diversity and importance of the achievements. With over two hundred new firsts and foremosts detailed in this book, Canadians continue to make their mark in significant ways.

There is much evidence that Canada is still wracked by a lack of confidence that impedes the country and its modest people from recognizing and trumpeting its own world leaders. As a result, surveys show, many Canadians (especially youth) are unaware of the achievements and many other key facts and figures in the country's history.

This lack of awareness has effects on every aspect of the country. Socially, the country, given its great size and relatively small popula-tion, lacks an adequate sense of community and civics that would give newcomers and natives alike a place of belonging and commit-ment. Politically, the country lacks leaders that put Canada first to resist the invasive and destructive forces of global corporatism. Economically, the country lacks corporations, especially financial institutions and venture capitalists, that believe in the nation and devote resources to supporting its growth as a self-reliant, self-sustaining community.

I have seen the negative effects of such self-deprecation in my own hometown in Connecticut, where the reasonable potential of the community was never realized. One of the further effects on a country, however, is a loss of national sovereignty as the direction of the country is determined more and more by forces outside its borders. The undermining influence of such international forces as the North American Free Trade Agreement (NAFTA) and the World Trade Organization (WTO) is only made more potent when, in their own minds, Canadians accept these influences as inevitable for such a "small" country.

This path of surrender is not inevitable, especially for a country such as Canada which, while relatively small in population, has produced so many world leaders in so many fields. The rest of the world, especially the United States, has benefited historically from this multi-varied Canadian originality and innovation. The likelihood that the creative spirit of Canada would dissipate if the country lost control of its own destiny should not be underestimated.

Canada Firsts and this book provide recognition for some of the best of Canada. Together, they are a small gift in return for what Canada has offered to the United States by way of wise paths to follow in areas such as health care, environmental protection, social services, consumer rights, and the arts. One benefit of the many wonderful visits I, and many other Americans, have made to many parts of Canada is an awareness of such pioneering achievements.

Ralph Nader
Washington, D.C.

ACKNOWLEDGEMENTS

This book would not have been written if Ralph Nader had not come up with the idea for *Canada Firsts: Ralph Nader's Salute to Canada and Canadian Achievement* in the 1980s. I had the privilege of working as a researcher and co-author on that book which, when published by McClelland & Stewart in 1992, became a number-one best-seller in Canada. Thank you, Ralph, for the opportunity to work on the first book, and for allowing me to extend your original idea with this collection.

Megan Poole helped get this second effort underway, sorting through the large file I had gathered over the past five years of clippings, notes, and citations about things that Canadians had done first or foremost in the world – things we missed in *Canada Firsts,* or that had occurred since the first book was published.

Chris Pullen played an invaluable role as researcher for the book, starting with basic information about each achievement and filling in the blanks in a very efficient, complete, and organized way. His enthusiasm and curiosity about the history of the widely varying accomplishments of Canadians were constantly helpful. I could not have written this book without his assistance. Near the end of the project, D'Arcy McLeish provided on short notice some necessary help in finishing research for the book, and his very effective assistance is greatly appreciated.

In addition, the hundreds of Canadians who responded to telephone calls and e-mails, or who maintain informative Web sites or whose books and articles aided our research, were, of course, invaluable sources of facts and figures about Canadian firsts and foremosts.

My parents, brothers, family members, friends, and Democracy Watch colleagues provide much-needed ongoing support, and without them I could not do the work that I do, including undertaking this book while Democracy Watch's activities continued at their usual overwhelming pace. Day-by-day work pressures often get in the way of thanking them as much as I want and letting them know how important their encouraging words, love, and friendship are to me.

McClelland & Stewart has remained interested and supportive of a second collection of Canadian firsts through the years, and without their generous and patient support this book would not have come to fruition. Alex Schultz, as editor, was also very patient, understanding, and helpful in completing the book.

The seed money from the proceeds of *Canada Firsts*, generously donated by Ralph Nader, allowed Democracy Watch to start up in the fall of 1993. The proceeds from *More Canada Firsts* will also be donated to Democracy Watch, helping it begin its seventh year of leading advocacy on issues of democratic reform, and government and corporate accountability in Canada.

Of course, while all of the people named above contributed in their own way to this book, any errors or omissions are my responsibility alone.

Duff Conacher, Coordinator
Democracy Watch
Ottawa

INTRODUCTION

The people of Canada, sprinkled across a vast landscape, have found an astounding array of ways to maintain contact with one another. They connect by radio, telephone, telegraph, the longest railway line in North America, and the longest highway and street in the world. They connect by kayak, canoe, by snowshoe or toboggan, by one of the oldest newspapers on the continent or by satellite.

Using snowmobiles, combines, jet aircraft, submarines, Laser sailboats, even hydrofoil boats, Canadians connect with one another. In every case, these connections have been made possible by the achievements or inventions of Canadians, or of the peoples who were here before the country was created, and are all firsts or foremosts in the world.

And what have we created through these connections? The best health-care system in the world, credit unions, YMCAs, public utilities, insulin, lacrosse, wheat that feeds the world, Greenpeace, ice hockey, the Canadarm, the National Film Board and the first documentary film, basketball, IMAX films, ginger ale, the first female lawyer and judge, football, the zipper, the green garbage bag, and automated tools. We've won gold medals, set world records, and executed unprecedented feats of athleticism on tracks, fields, courts, ski slopes, on ice skates, and in the water. And, of course, we achieved the unprecedented by gaining independence from the Empire without a revolution. The stories behind all these firsts or foremosts in the world, and many others, are told in the 1992 book *Canada Firsts*.

And now here is *More Canada Firsts*, a collection of over 200 more Canadian individuals and institutions that have achieved a first or foremost in the world. What is the story these achievements tell? First, they confirm that Canada is not just another stripe on the U.S. flag, nor just another star. (But if we were, we would be one of its brightest stars. For from a population a bit less than the state of California, we have produced a truly amazing list of achievements.)

Second, they demonstrate not only that Canadians dream of achieving great things as much as anyone, but also that many people fulfill their dreams by coming to Canada. Our historically welcoming arms have provided great benefits to the country and the world, for over thirty of the firsts and foremosts in this book were achieved by immigrants, and many more by first-generation Canadians.

Third, they show that Canadians continue to prove their ingenuity, distinctiveness, diversity, and persistent patriotism in a wide variety of fields. Beyond the achievements listed in this book, we can find other evidence of our nationhood in such things as the 2,000 Canadianisms found in the *Canadian Oxford Dictionary*, words and phrases such as aboriginal rights, bush party, butter tart (also a Canadian creation), grain elevator manager, house league, ice-fishing hut, lake boat, north of 60, out-of-province, parks officer, peace bond, registry office, stickhandle, and wheat pool, along with, of course, the numerous linguistic creations of francophones across Canada.

Perhaps most importantly, however, there is lots of evidence in this book that we provide less support for our dreamers than do many countries. Our governments frequently neglect scientific researchers and artists, our banks show little imagination or flexibility when dealing with entrepreneurs and innovative, job-creating companies, and as a society we often knock down people who rise above the crowd.

There are numerous inventors and businesspeople who sought private financing in Canada, only to be turned away by the big banks and other financial institutions, including venture capital firms. How many more new businesses have been pushed out of the country by lack of imaginative and flexible financial support? This is not to say that the people who control the flow of capital in Canada are not innovative. They show great imagination in finding ways to invest in money markets, commodities markets, securities markets, and countless derivatives of these markets. But when it comes to supporting industrial innovation and making real investments, as *Canada Firsts* and *More Canada Firsts* both show time and again, our capitalists are unimaginative, unsupportive, and lagging behind governments. Ironically, these capitalists call on government to get out of the way of innovation and technological development.

With all the recent calls by big-business executives for lower taxes and smaller government, readers may be surprised at how hard it is to find an achievement in this book that was accomplished without some sort of financial support from government. The National Research Council and the National Sciences and Engineering Research Council alone provided key funding for thirteen world-leading scientific achievements detailed in this book. Those entrepreneurs who did not receive direct support, benefited – and along with many large businesses still benefit – from indirect support through tax deductions or credits for research, exploration and development, government counselling and support services for fledgling and export businesses, and (no less important) through use of our public health-care, roadways, electricity, water and other public services.

Despite these ongoing contributions, there is evidence that government funding supporting innovation and leaders is inadequate and not always handed out in a fair and effective manner. Too often, donations to political parties and the undue influence of corporate lobbyists determine the flow of government cash, instead of the merits of a funding proposal or contract bid. Clearly, our governments and capitalists can do better at supporting, documenting, and promoting the best of the country. Beyond the entrepreneurs mentioned above, many other Canadians have had to go elsewhere for support. For example, twelve scientists whose achievements are documented in this book, including four Nobel Prize winners, should not have had to leave Canada to find funding to pursue their research. And we should not have lost control of Spar Aerospace, including its space robotics division (which created the Canadarm for the National Research Council for use on NASA's space shuttle, as detailed in *Canada Firsts*), nor RADARSAT International (which produces the world's most powerful commercial Earth observation satellite, as detailed in this book) to American companies.

How can governments and corporations provide fair and adequate support and recognition for deserving Canadians and Canadian companies involved in activities that help grow a diverse, distinct, world-leading and self-reliant economy and society? First, government loan and grant programs of departments and Crown financial institutions, such as the Business Development Bank of Canada, should be increased. To ensure that these programs support real investment and the development of innovative, job-creating industries, there should be public disclosure requirements for applicants, strict conflict-of-interest rules, citizen oversight boards, and a regular audit of the programs.

Tax credits should also be introduced to encourage real investment by companies (especially investment that fuels innovation and job-creating growth), while the many tax subsidies that encourage speculative investments in the stock market (which do little to support innovation and industrial development, especially those that encourage investments in other countries) should be eliminated.

Loans, grants, and tax breaks from government can help companies undertake job-creating and innovative research and development, but even more necessary is to ensure financial institutions, especially banks, fulfill their primary purpose of providing capital. Our big five banks lend five times more each year than the combined spending of federal, provincial, and territorial governments. If the capital these and other financial institutions control is not directed toward real investment in our economy (and there is much evidence that currently it is not), we will be caught in a downward economic spiral that drains cash out of the country and takes our world leaders in a wide variety of fields with it.

Our governments should enact requirements for detailed disclosure by financial institutions of their loans to, and investments in, individuals, businesses, and community development projects, along with a regular audit to determine if they are supporting creditworthy applicants and penalties if they have a poor record. Such measures, enacted more than twenty years ago in the United States, would help ensure that Canadian capital supports Canadians.

This book also contains many examples of academic–business partnership, with the development, in the early 1970s, of QUICKLAW at Queen's University and Sciex's mass spectrometer technology at the University of Toronto being probably the first examples (see also, among others, the V-chip and light-activated drugs). Such partnerships were controversial then, and remain controversial in terms of maintaining a separation between public-funded institutions and private, for-profit businesses, and ensuring that professors adhere to academic, as opposed to private sector, principles in their scholarship and teaching. Clearly written laws on partnerships between public institutions and private businesses would help ensure that these partnerships are always undertaken in the public interest.

Other innovations noted in this book are spurred on by the demands of the military, such as the invention of the gyro-stabilized and 3-D camera systems, both originally developed for battlefield observation. Such inventions, of course, raise questions about how and why we are able to find financing to support the research and development of technology for military uses, but cannot support innovations for use in peacetime.

More opportunities for all citizens to participate in all aspects of society is another important goal if we want to encourage world leaders. Today, someone like Sam Langford, born in Nova Scotia in the late 1800s, would not be barred from boxing professionally because he was black, and perhaps would be given a chance to show he was possibly one of the best boxers ever. Still, many people in Canada, especially women and visible minorities, face formal or informal barriers to full participation in society, and to pursuing their dreams.

We do not have to wait for all the measures above to be enacted, however, before undertaking a full review to determine whether the type of businesses we publicly support (and that private financial institutions support) adhere to the criteria of sustainable development. Such a review can only help prevent us from perpetuating business and industrial sectors that impose more costs on our society than benefits.

It is important to note that even if government funding and contracting-out processes are cleaned up and only deserving companies, artists, and athletes receive funding, our governments will still not be able to develop every Canadian with potential into a world leader. For example, artists and athletes have left the country in part because the audiences and teams that will allow them to reach their world-beating status are elsewhere. No government (or corporation) can create in Canada the millions of fans and sports leagues needed to support all these achievers.

There are also steps that should be avoided if we want to support world-leading developments. Most importantly, no government should react to the much-hyped (but unproven) claims of a critical "brain-drain" from Canada by adopting massive personal income tax cuts. This seemingly simple solution has many more costs than benefits, and is also unjustified. As several analyses have shown, after-tax purchasing power in Canadian cities is comparable to that in many U.S. cities. And these comparisons usually do not take into account the priceless peace of mind most Canadians enjoy thanks to our low crime rate and ease of access to high-quality health care, among other social goods.

In terms of recognizing Canadian achievement, flag giveaways and other symbolic government programs to boost national identity do little to help in any substantive way. Where are the initiatives dedicated to educating the public about Canadian firsts and foremosts, among other key episodes of our past? There are signs of improvement since *Canada Firsts* was published in late 1992, such as the new National Research Council Achievement Awards for scientists, the new Walk of Fame in Toronto for artists and entertainers, and the new Entrepreneur of the Year awards by the Business Development

Bank of Canada. As well, six compilation books have been published since 1992 celebrating wide-ranging Canadian achievements, including one documenting the neglected area of the history of women inventors. This matches the total number of such books published in Canada in the twenty-five years preceding 1992.

However, while there have been some advances to aid research for a book of this sort (most notably the Internet), it is still amazingly difficult to track down Canadian firsts and foremosts in the world. (Any readers who know of such first or foremosts are invited to send details to me care of McClelland & Stewart.) And the history of Canadian achievements remains largely unknown to many Canadians. Without this knowledge it is impossible to make wise choices about where support should be directed to create the conditions needed to produce future world leaders in any field.

This book, following in the footsteps of *Canada Firsts*, is intended to provide some of this crucial documenting and promotion. To the extent that it also provides evidence of how these firsts and foremosts were achieved and some of their positive effects on Canada and the world, it will perhaps help the country choose a wise path in the future.

As with any effort to determine firsts and foremosts, the achievements detailed in this book raise issues and questions. First, to be clear, this book is a compilation of firsts and foremosts Canadians have achieved in the world, not firsts in Canada or firsts in North America or the Western world.

Second, it is becoming more difficult to determine the "Canadianness" of many achievements as the world's population becomes more and more mobile. Whether Canadians are going to the United States or elsewhere to achieve their distinctions, or people from other countries are coming here to do the same, questions arise as to which country can legitimately claim credit. Also, in many fields it continues to be difficult even to measure firsts and foremosts, most notably in the arts. Many of our artists are certainly worthy of recognition, but in what way can we determine they are clearly first or foremost?

Finally, there are of course disputes over whether a particular achievement is a first or foremost in the world. For example, is Canada actually one of the first officially bilingual countries in the world? Was the fountain pen actually invented in Canada? And is the World's Biggest Bookstore in Toronto actually the world's biggest? (Not according to the *Guinness Book of World Records*, but maybe depending on how you count shelf space.)

Beyond documenting many clear Canadian firsts and foremosts in the world, and others that may raise some of the issues and questions set out above, this book will hopefully provoke consideration of what we celebrate, and what we neglect, and why. For as we head into the next millennium as a relative infant among industrialized countries, Canada has more growing up to do. And considering such issues is part of the process of maturing as a society. For our own good, and the good of the world, our growth to maturity should come with the realization that self-confidence is not the same thing as arrogance, celebration of achievements is not the same as jingoism, and knowing our own history does not mean we will close our eyes to the world.

HISTORICAL ACHIEVEMENTS

LAW SOCIETY OF UPPER CANADA
WORLD'S FIRST STATUTORY LAWYERS' GOVERNING BODY

On July 17, 1797, ten of the fifteen lawyers then practising in Upper Canada, now Ontario, met at Wilson's Inn at Niagara-on-the-Lake. At the meeting, they founded the Law Society of Upper Canada, the world's first self-governing association of lawyers. John White, the eldest member at age thirty-six, was Attorney General of the province at the time, and he was elected as the first Treasurer (similar to a president) of the Law Society. Half of the lawyers in attendance at the founding meeting were under thirty, and one was nineteen.

The Law Society of Upper Canada's purpose, then and now, is to regulate admission to the legal profession (known as being "called to the bar") and ensure that those called to the bar follow proper procedures and ethics. In 1897, it became the first bar in the British Empire to admit a woman to the profession. That year, Clara Brett Martin, who had campaigned since 1891 for changes to rules preventing her from studying and practising law, was finally approved for entry to the profession by a twelve to eleven vote of the benchers (representatives) in Convocation (as the ruling body of the Law Society is known – see story in *Canada Firsts*).

The Law Society of Upper Canada is the largest in Canada, with over 27,000 members. Although the words Upper Canada are no longer used to describe Ontario, the benchers of the Law Society recently voted to maintain not only the original name of the Society, but also the titles of Treasurer and bencher, and the name Convocation for its ruling body. Though obscure for modern Ontarians (including many lawyers) these terms connect lawyers of today with their visionary forebears whose self-regulating model has been followed by other provinces, U.S. states, and jurisdictions in many other countries.

THE *MARCO POLO*
WORLD'S FASTEST SHIP IN THE 1850s

The *Marco Polo* was built in Saint John, New Brunswick, in April 1851. A 1,625-tonne ship, it was a cross between a cargo ship and a yacht. The day the *Marco Polo* was launched its size and weight propelled it across the harbour and beached it on a mud shoal opposite the dry docks. It is speculated that the collision with the shoal reshaped the hull and accounted for the *Marco Polo's* legendary speed.

This hybrid design proved to be a fortuitous one. The *Marco Polo's* first crossing of the Atlantic took only fifteen days. The record crossing at the time for a sailing ship was fourteen days. The ship was bought and converted to a luxury liner by the Blackball Line of Australia. Its first voyage from Liverpool to Australia was a record outward run of sixty-eight days and a record round trip of five months and twenty-one days. Based on this trip, the *Marco Polo* came to be considered the fastest sailing ship in the world of its day.

The ship was damaged by a collision with an iceberg in 1861 and finished its career as a tramp cargo ship. It eventually ran aground off Cavendish, Prince Edward Island, on July 22, 1883. Speculation abounded that the owners were committing a fraud to collect insurance on the ship. An interesting note was that the only eyewitness account of the collision was written by an eight-year-old girl. Her story went on to win some local prizes for literature and was eventually published by the *Montreal Gazette*. It was the first published work of Lucy Maud Montgomery, who went on to become a journalist and to write *Anne of Green Gables* and many other books.

FIRST LABOUR DAY

Contrary to the popular notion that Peter J. McGuire, one of the founders of the American Federation of Labor (now the AFL-CIO), is the "Father of Labour Day," Canadian trade unionists actually organized the first day of celebration on April 15, 1872. About 10,000 Torontonians turned out for the "workingman's demonstration" and to listen to speeches calling for the abolition of the law that stated that trade unions were criminal conspiracies that restricted trade. A similar demonstration was held in Ottawa on September 3 of that year. At the event, Prime Minister Sir John A. Macdonald pledged to union leaders that his government would repeal the conspiracy laws, and it did so that fall.

Over the next decade, the Toronto Trades and Labour Council held an annual labour demonstration and picnic. In 1882, Peter J. McGuire was invited to come from New York to speak at the event held that year on July 22. On his return to the U.S., McGuire suggested to the New York Central Labor Union that they also set aside an annual festive day for a demonstration and picnic.

Meanwhile, in Canada, pressure from labour organizations resulted in Parliament, led by Prime Minister Sir John Thompson, passing a law on July 23, 1894, declaring that a day be set aside to celebrate those who labour. May 1 was briefly recognized as Labour Day in Canada, but it was later changed to September so that the holiday coincided with the end of the summer. In Europe, Labour Day was first celebrated later than in Canada, but was officially recognized earlier, on May 1, 1886.

Harriet Brooks
FIRST FEMALE NUCLEAR PHYSICIST

Harriet Brooks was born in Exeter, Ontario, on July 2, 1876. She did her undergraduate studies on a scholarship at McGill University, studying in 1898 with physicist Ernest Rutherford, who went on to win a Nobel Prize for chemistry in 1908.

Brooks continued into graduate studies, eventually pursuing a Ph.D. in physics at Bryn Mawr College. During her Ph.D. studies in 1901, Brooks played an important role in the discovery of radioactivity. Her study of emanation (now known as radon) showed that the substance was a gas with very different properties than radium. This discovery provided the first evidence that one element can change into another, and made her a leader in this scientific field. Brooks was also the first person to try and determine the atomic mass on radon, and the first woman to study at the Cavendish Laboratory at Cambridge University, England (on a fellowship in 1902–1903).

With her Ph.D., Brooks later tutored physics at Columbia University's college for women. Her engagement to Frank Pitcher created controversy at the school, and when they were married in 1907 she was forced to give up her professional scientific work. They settled in Montreal and raised three children. Brooks remained active in the Canadian Federation of University Women through her life, and died April 17, 1933.

The *Bluenose*
FASTEST SCHOONER OF ITS TIME

In 1920 Senator William Denise, publisher of the *Halifax Herald*, initiated a series of races to determine the fastest boat in the American and Canadian fishing fleets. In the first year the series was won by an American boat from Gloucester, Massachusetts.

In response to the results of the first race, Angus Walters undertook to build a schooner to challenge the Americans. With help from friends, he sold 350 shares at one hundred dollars apiece to raise the money needed to design and build the ship. Designed by Halifax marine architect William J. Roue (with modifications suggested by Walters) and built in Lunenburg, Nova Scotia, the *Bluenose* was launched on March 26, 1921. Deep-bellied and with a spoon-shaped bow, the forty-three-metre *Bluenose* won the International Fisherman's Cup in her first race that year – and for the next seventeen years. In the schooner's final race, on October 26, 1938, the *Bluenose* led the U.S. *Gertrude L. Thebaud* in the tie-breaking race of the five-race series. A key piece of the sail rigging failed close to the finish line, but with Walters urging her on from the helm, the *Bluenose* held off the American challenger, and was awarded the Cup forever in recognition of her amazing string of victories.

The *Bluenose* also holds the record for the single largest catch of fish ever landed at Lunenburg. Eventually, the creditors that financed the *Bluenose* couldn't keep up with the cost of maintaining the ship. Angus Walters mortgaged his dairy farm to try and buy the schooner back from the creditors, but it was instead sold to a West Indies trading company. While in the service of this company, the *Bluenose* wrecked on a reef off Haiti and was abandoned.

In 1963, a replica of the boat, the *Bluenose II*, was christened at Lunenburg, and Angus Walters was named Honorary Captain.

LE CHÂTEAU MONTEBELLO
WORLD'S LARGEST LOG BUILDING

The original idea for Le Château Montebello was put forth by H. M. Saddlemire, a Swiss-American. Saddlemire had already built a similar, but smaller, building in Maine, called the Lucerne-in-Maine, as a private club. Montebello was originally to be called the "Lucerne-in-Quebec" and the club was to be called the Lucerne-in-Quebec Community Association Limited.

However, when the Montebello project was undertaken by the Canadian Pacific Railway, it ended up as the private "Seignory Club." Excavation on the foundation started on March 15, 1930. The first log was placed on April 7, 1930, and the log work was done by June 7, 1930, with other construction work completed by the official opening on July 1, 1930. In just three months, the workers had built the world's largest log building.

Montebello was designed by Montreal architect Harold Lawson, and its construction was directed by Victor Nymark from Finland, who was considered the world's greatest log builder. A special 1,110-metre-long extension of the main railway line in the area was built to bring in 100,000 red cedar logs from British Columbia. Four rail cars of logs were unloaded each day and by the end 1,200 cars had been delivered to the site.

At the height of construction 3,500 men worked ten- to twelve-hour shifts to complete the main Montebello buildings in time. General labourers made twenty cents an hour and first-class carpenters made fifty-five cents an hour, and they worked mainly with hand tools. Most of the log construction was completed by workers of Scandinavian descent who were familiar with Nymark's work.

Not surprisingly, the world's largest log building boasts other impressive construction statistics: 85 kilometres of plumbing and heating materials, 64 kilometres of electrical wiring, 7,600 sprinkler heads, 1,400 doors, 535 windows, and 166 kilometres of wooden moulding. Le Château Montebello is now owned by Canadian Pacific Hotels.

THE DIONNE SISTERS
FIRST QUINTUPLETS KNOWN TO SURVIVE INFANCY

On May 28, 1934, in Corbeil, Ontario, five identical baby girls emerged into the world, two months premature and weighing less than two pounds each: Annette, Cecile, Emilie, Marie, and Yvonne. The Dionne quintuplets, as they were soon known, quickly became international celebrities as the first quintuplets to survive infancy.

Unfortunately, their fame led the Ontario government and others to treat them like a commercial product. They were taken away from their parents and placed under the supervision of Dr. Allan Roy Dafoe, who had delivered them, in a display house called "Quintland," across from their parents' home. There, up to 6,000 people came each day to watch them play through a one-way viewing window. Dr. Dafoe also arranged product endorsement agreements with hundreds of companies.

In 1943, after a legal battle, their parents regained custody of the quintuplets. Two of the sisters died at quite young ages, Emilie in 1954, and Marie in 1970. Annette, Cecile, and Yvonne live in the suburbs of Montreal. In 1995, they went public with an allegation that their father had sexually abused them over several years. In 1998, they settled a lawsuit for millions of dollars against the Ontario government for a share of the earnings the province made from the quintuplets' tourist-attraction home.

DAVID ADIE
FIRST PERSON TO RUN THE GREAT WALL OF CHINA

In 1982, David Adie made a promise to a young boy that they would run the Great Wall of China together to inspire other youth to overcome obstacles in life and fulfill their dreams. Unfortunately, the young boy who came up with the idea took his own life in 1988 before he and Adie could undertake the challenge. Years of delays, many imposed by the Chinese government, meant that Adie had to wait until 1994 for an opportunity to attempt the run.

Born September 13, 1958, in Calgary, Alberta, Adie grew up in a large family. He studied dance when he was quite young, and remembers the generosity of the instructor who offered him lessons for free because he knew that it would make it easier for Adie's parents who had many expenses raising their children. Adie always loved running, and trained with the goal of making the Canadian team for the 1980 Summer Olympics. However, that dream was derailed when Canada, along with many other countries, boycotted the Moscow Olympics in protest against the invasion of Afghanistan by the U.S.S.R.

In 1979 and 1980, Adie worked for Canada World Youth, leading a group of Canadian youth on a posting in Malaysia. The experience gave him an appreciation of the benefits of cross-cultural communication and education. From there, he became a teacher in

Vancouver, and also worked with youth with learning and social difficulties. One day he was talking with one of the boys he worked with about overcoming barriers, and they came up with the idea of overcoming the largest human-made obstacle on Earth by running the length of the Great Wall.

Over the next several years, Adie worked as an acting and dance instructor for kids, while also acting and dancing himself. His promise slipped to the back of his mind, and then one day he heard that the boy had committed suicide. It shocked Adie and made him realize that he had not focused on accomplishing the dream he had shared with the boy, and he resolved not to let anything else prevent him from running the Wall.

One of the obstacles Adie had to overcome was very personal, and almost stopped him from running altogether. In early January 1990, Adie was paralyzed by a rare neuro-muscular disease, Guillain-Barre Syndrome. As a result, and in defiance of predictions by his doctors who told him he should expect to die, Adie spent the next year and a half relearning how to talk and walk, let alone run.

And run he did when the chance finally came. He overcame obstacles created by the Chinese government, who did not want their public claim that the run was impossible proven false. The Chinese government gave him inaccurate maps, delayed him midway through his run by asking him to pay upfront the various costs they had imposed for permission to attempt the run, and then disbanded his Chinese support team. This obstructionism led many of Adie's sponsors, including the Canadian government, to abandon him, even though he still intended to complete the run. The sponsors assumed now that he would fail in his attempt, and since the run was considered important to Chinese–Canadian relations, they began trying to downplay the importance of the attempt.

However, Adie and his younger brother Richard pressed on alone, with minimal resources and financing. They were arrested four times, and almost shot, in the last month of the run, but all of these hurdles, and the wearing out of seven pairs of running shoes, did not stop Adie from keeping his promise by covering the

5,000-kilometre distance in an amazingly short ninety-nine days, from July 1 to October 7, 1994.

Since Adie completed his run, the Chinese government has reversed its position and officially recognized his feat. A TV documentary about his run, "The Great Run of China," was viewed by close to one billion people in China, and has also been shown in Canada.

Adie has not rested on the laurels of his world first, however. Since then he has run 3,000 kilometres in Japan in July–August 1995, 6,000 kilometres through Singapore, Hong Kong, and the Philippines between December 1996 and March 1997, and 3,000 kilometres in Great Britain and Ireland in 1997. All along the way, Adie has shared his experiences of overcoming obstacles with youth, making presentations to more than 300,000 young people in seventeen countries through the "Yes I Can" Children's Foundation International and the "Steps 2 Peace" International Peace Initiative for Children.

In the late summer of 1999, Adie set off to Austrailia from his home in Calgary, for a planned 5,000-kilometre run through the outback from Brisbane on the east coast to Perth on the west coast, with many presentations to youth planned to follow his run. The run will raise funds for the Australian Teenage Cancer Patients Society (CANTEEN), a charitable organization created and guided by teenagers living with cancer.

MARIE LOUISE MEILLEUR (NÉE CHASSE)
WORLD'S OLDEST LIVING PERSON

Was it her upbringing in rural Quebec? Her meatless diet? The hand-rolled cigarettes she smoked into her nineties? The twelve children she gave birth to? Or her eighty-five grandchildren, eighty great-grandchildren, fifty-seven great-great-grandchildren, and four great-great-great-grandchildren? Though we can only guess at the secret to her longevity, it's a fact that Marie Louise Meilleur became the world's oldest living person before her death at age 117 on April 27, 1998 (she was not the oldest person ever).

Meilleur was born in Kamouraska, Quebec, to Pierre Chasse and Febronie Lévesque on August 29, 1880, when Canada was only thirteen years old. She grew up in this small community west of Rivière-du-Loup, Quebec. At age nineteen, she married a fisherman, Gerald Leclair, and they had six children (sadly, two died at birth). Unfortunately, Gerald died of pneumonia, and afterwards Meilleur moved to Rapide-des-Joachims, in west Quebec. While there she married Hector Meilleur, who already had four children, and together they had six more. Hector had a long life himself, dying in 1972 at age ninety-four.

Meilleur died from a blood clot in her lung at the Nipissing Manor seniors' home, in Corbeil, Ontario. Originally built for the Dionne quintuplets (see "The Dionne Sisters" above), the home is fifteen kilometres southeast of North Bay.

UNITED NATIONS NAMES CANADA AS BEST COUNTRY FOR HUMAN DEVELOPMENT

Since 1990, the United Nations Development Programme (UNDP) has published annual Human Development Reports. They began as reports on a few countries, but now rank 175 countries in a comprehensive guide to global human development. The reports define human development as more than growth in income or the Gross National Product of any country. Included in the definition are factors considered critical to living a long and healthy life, being educated, and having access to resources needed for a decent standard of living. All of these factors are considered in the calculation of UNDP's Human Development Index, with the recognition that any country's ranking reflects national averages, not details about individual lives, and that many factors in human development such as political freedoms and guaranteed protection of human rights are very difficult to quantify.

Since 1990, countries have been ranked according to the extent to which they create a conducive environment for people, individually and collectively, to develop their full potential in accordance with their needs and interests. While Japan was ranked first overall in 1990, 1991, and 1993, Canada was ranked first in 1992, and from 1994 to 1999, consistently above the U.S., Japan, France, the Netherlands, Iceland, Norway, Finland, and Sweden, whose ranking order changed slightly each year. Each year's report is usually based upon three-year-old statistics so, for example, Canada's 1999 ranking was based on 1996 statistics.

The reports have revealed some compelling conclusions, such as that the link between economic growth and human progress is not automatic, and inversely that at a relatively low national income level human development can progress quite well. Also, that a participatory approach that includes the involvement of non-governmental organizations is crucial for any human development strategy to be successful. In addition, the reports have detailed an ongoing gap between the many opportunities for development offered to men, and the relatively few opportunities offered to women. Closing this gap is considered to be essential to worldwide human development.

To address key gaps more directly, the Human Development Reports have added a Human Poverty Index (HPI), a Gender-related Development Index (GDI), and a Gender Empowerment Measure (GEM) in recent years. These indices reveal details of country rankings not highlighted in the main index. Despite its first overall ranking in 1999, for example, Canada ranked fourth in the gender-related index and ninth out of the seventeen richest industrialized countries in the poverty index.

TRANSPORTATION

THE QUEBEC BRIDGE
WORLD'S LONGEST CANTILEVER BRIDGE

In 1900, construction began on a bridge that would set a world record, but also record two disasters along the way. The Quebec Bridge was almost finished on August 29, 1907, when its southern span collapsed, killing seventy-five men, many of them from the Caughnawaga native band. It was Canada's worst bridge disaster, attributed by the results of an inquiry to faulty design and inadequate supervision.

On September 11, 1916, a new centre span was being hoisted into position when it fell and killed thirteen men. Finally finished in 1917, the 1,800-metre-long bridge was officially opened by the Prince of Wales (later Edward VIII) on August 22, 1919. It was the longest cantilever bridge in the world at that time.

PUNCH DICKINS
FIRST TO FLY THE BARREN LANDS OF CANADA'S
NORTHWEST TERRITORIES

Clennell Haggerston "Punch" Dickins was born in Portage la Prairie, Manitoba, on January 12, 1899, just four years before Wilbur and Orville Wright made their pioneering flights in their airplane. Dickins grew up in Edmonton, Alberta, and at age seventeen enlisted for service in the First World War, soon flying airplanes himself for the Royal Flying Corps. During his seven-month tour in France he shot down seven enemy aircraft, earning the Distinguished Flying Cross for gallantry.

From 1921 to 1927, Dickins served in the Royal Canadian Air Force, tested various aircraft under winter conditions, flew forestry patrols, and conducted photographic surveys. After his service he joined Western Canadian Airways and began his pioneering flights in Canada's north.

Dickins flew many prospectors north over the years, including miner Gilbert LaBine when he made the discovery of silver, copper, and pitchblende (an ore containing uranium and radium) on the cliffs of Echo Bay on Great Bear Lake. LaBine's discovery led to the opening of the Eldorado Mine, which extracted raw materials used to helped establish Canada's nuclear industry.

In August 1928, Dickins flew a prospecting party on a twelve-day trip that totalled almost 6,499 kilometres over the Barren Lands of Canada's Northwest Territories, from Chesterfield Inlet on Hudson Bay to the western side of Lake Athabasca in Saskatchewan. This area was virtually uncharted, and Dickins had to fly mainly by sight as the proximity of the magnetic pole made compass navigation unreliable. It was an amazing achievement, as those who have flown over tundra can attest, because from the air the tundra is a uniform landscape with little vegetation or wildlife.

In January 1929, Dickins became the first pilot for a northern mail service for winter delivery to northern communities. Up to that point mail traditionally arrived in these remote communities only once or twice a winter by dog sled. Dickins's first deliveries were greeted enthusiastically throughout the north as they helped alleviate some of the isolation of life in these communities. As documented in *Canada Firsts*, Dickins's achievements were not the only Canadian "firsts and foremosts" in northern aviation, as in 1935–36 in Montreal Robert Noorduyn began to design and manufacture the Norseman aircraft, which became one of the most widely used northern bush aircraft in the world.

During the Second World War, Dickins managed six flight training schools that were part of the British Commonwealth Air Training Plan. After the war he joined de Havilland Aircraft as director, where he played a key role in the marketing of the Canadian-made Beaver bush aircraft worldwide. Dickins was named an Officer of the Order of the British Empire in 1936 and an Officer of the Order of Canada in 1968. He died in 1995 at the age of ninety-six.

THE RCMP *ST. ROCH*
FIRSTS IN SHIPPING

In the early 1940s, the Canadian government wanted to establish a police force to patrol the Arctic Northwest Passage, the Eastern Arctic, and Allied interests in Greenland. A ship could have travelled south and through the Panama Canal, but there was fear that such a voyage would be vulnerable to German U-boat attack.

Instead, the RCMP *St. Roch,* a wooden, sail-powered schooner with a back-up engine, headed north from Victoria in 1940, and completed the first west to east crossing of the 7,500-mile Northwest Passage when it finally arrived in Halifax in 1942. The ship was forced to remain in the Arctic over the winter twice, lodging in remote coves along the Arctic coast. During the winter months the ship's officers, led by skipper Henry Larsen, a native of Norway who had become a Canadian citizen in 1927, carried out patrols by dog sled.

On July 22, 1944, the *St. Roch* left Dartmouth, Nova Scotia, to undertake an east to west crossing of the Passage. With its arrival in Vancouver on October 16 that same year, the ship became the first to accomplish the trip in a single year. Norwegian explorer Roald Amundsen was the first to traverse the Passage east to west in his ship the *Gjoa,* but it had taken him four years, from 1903 to 1906. Ironically, Amundsen's exploits inspired Henry Larsen to explore the Arctic.

Six years later, on March 6, 1950, the *St. Roch* left Esquimalt, B.C., heading south, and arrived via the Panama Canal in Halifax on May 29, 1950. With this voyage, the ship became the first to circumnavigate

North America. Sergeant F. S. (Ted) Farrar, who travelled on both the northern and southern trips, became the first person to have sailed completely around North America.

The first ship to cross the Passage from west to east in the same year was the Canadian government icebreaker *Labrador,* in 1954.

DR. ELIZABETH "ELSIE" GREGORY MacGILL
FIRST WOMAN TO DESIGN FIGHTER AND TRANSPORT PLANES

Elizabeth "Elsie" Gregory MacGill was born in Vancouver, B.C., in 1905 to James MacGill and Helen Gregory MacGill, one of Canada's first female judges. MacGill would take a different career path than her mother, but one similarly pioneering. Studying at the University of Toronto, she was the first woman to receive an electrical engineering degree in Canada. MacGill went on to receive her doctorate at the Massachusetts Institute of Technology in 1929, making her the first woman to obtain an engineering degree from that institution, and the first woman in North America to hold a degree in aeronautical engineering.

After working at Fairchild Aircraft Ltd. in Longueil, Quebec, in 1938 MacGill was appointed chief engineer at the Canadian Car and Foundry company in Montreal, the first woman in North America to ever hold such a position.

During the Second World War, MacGill became the first female aircraft designer in the world. She designed and supervised production of the winterized version of the famous Hawker Hurricane, the first fighter plane to have skis and de-icing equipment. She also created the Maple Leaf II, a training plane for the Mexican Air Force, which is probably the only plane ever completely designed by a woman. The plane went from design stage to air worthiness certification in eight months, which was a record at the time.

Because she had suffered poliomyelitis as a child, MacGill had to walk with a cane, and couldn't fly the planes she designed. However, she joined the pilots on all test flights of aircraft she worked on, including the first flight, which, for obvious reasons, is the most dangerous.

In 1946, MacGill became the first female technical advisor to the UN's International Civil Aviation Organization, helping to draft international airworthiness regulations for commercial aircraft. She was also the first female member of both the Canadian Aeronautical and Space institute and the Engineering Institute of Canada, the winner of many engineering awards, and an advocate for the rights of women and children. MacGill died in 1980.

JERRY WRIGHT
INVENTOR OF COMPUTER NAVIGATION SYSTEM

Jerry Wright was born August 31, 1917, in Liverpool, Nova Scotia, and he went on to navigate many other parts of the world, aided by his own inventions. After finishing high school, Wright studied to become a pharmaceutical clerk, and worked at a drugstore in Liverpool for a few years. He entered the Royal Canadian Air Force in 1940 as a lowest-rank AC 2 trainee navigator, but he was promoted to corporal after basic training and was a sergeant by the time he was shipped to Greenock, Scotland, in December.

Wright had taken a celestial navigation course at an Air Force base in Canada, and after a few more weeks' training in Scotland, he was placed as a navigator with the so-called "flying boats" that flew missions across the ocean up to thirty-two hours long. Navigators at the time used the sun and the stars to provide bearings, or in bad weather used wind velocity gauges, dead reckoning, and hunches to determine the direction and length of a flight.

After just under two years patrolling for enemy submarines along the northern European coastline, Wright was shifted to an Air Force base in Madras, India. His experience with all the available navigational tools and his improvement of a navigational guide earned him a promotion to flight lieutenant.

In 1944, Wright began working with eight other navigational experts on a review of navigational systems. This review led to his invention and design of the R-Theta computer, a machine that fit into the small fighter plane cockpit and continuously displayed the location and distance from home base. The R-Theta (the "R" stands for "range," and "Theta" means "angle") eliminated the need for the pilot to rely on ground radio to direct the plane home. Often guidance from the ground was interrupted by radio jamming systems used by opposing forces, and so the computer system helped many cut-off pilots return home.

The R-Theta computer remained an air-navigation standard until the 1970s when it was replaced by super-high-precision gyroscopic technology, which was also eventually replaced by satellite systems. Jerry Wright holds thirty patents in the area of navigation tools and construction. Since he was in the armed services when he developed the R-Theta computer, the Canadian government has received all the royalties from sales of that system.

WORLD'S FIRST FEMALE JET FIGHTER PILOTS

The Canadian Forces opened all sectors of the armed forces to women in the late 1980s except the Submarine division. Deanna Brasseur (now a Major) had joined the military when she was nineteen years old, working initially as a typist. In 1979, she began training as a pilot.

Through the 1980s, Brasseur recorded milestones such as becoming the first woman in the Canadian military to be a flight instructor, senior course director, and deputy flight commander. Both she and Jane Foster (now a Captain) were Tudor jet instructors at Canadian Forces Base (CFB) Moose Jaw. They faced many challenges trying to break into the male-dominated world of the military, and the jet fighter pilot program in particular, including discrimination and alienation.

In the mid 1980s, Brasseur and Foster were trained and certified at CFB Cold Lake, Alberta on the CF-5 aircraft, and then moved on to CF-18 Hornets, considered to be among the premier fighter jets in the world. On February 17, 1989, they became the first two women in the world to fly CF-18s. Almost thirty years earlier, on February 20, 1959, Prime Minister John Diefenbaker announced that Canada's

Avro Arrow program was being cancelled. The Arrow was hailed at the time as perhaps the most advanced jet fighter plane in the world (see story in *Canada Firsts*).

The Netherlands was the first country to allow women to fly in regular service and the first woman in the world qualified there for jet fighter training in a CF-16, but she did not complete training before Brasseur and Foster. Canada was the second country to allow women to fly in regular operations.

Brasseur has logged 2,500 hours in CF-18s. An injury that damaged the nerves in her elbow forced her out of flying, and she retired from the Air Force. Foster now flies helicopters out of CFB Moose Jaw.

THE CONFEDERATION BRIDGE
WORLD'S LONGEST CONTINUOUS MARINE-SPAN BRIDGE

The 12.9-kilometre-long Confederation Bridge, which spans the Northumberland Strait at its narrowest point between Borden–Carleton, Prince Edward Island, and Jourimain, New Brunswick, is the world's longest continuous marine-span bridge over ice-covered waters.

After much controversy, a plebiscite in which Islanders voted 60 per cent in favour of the bridge, and after almost four years and one billion dollars were spent in its construction, the bridge opened May 31, 1997. It carries two lanes of traffic twenty-four hours a day and can be crossed in about ten minutes if conditions are good. The bridge is deliberately curved to keep drivers focused on driving, in the hope that this will reduce accidents.

The bridge was built by Strait Crossing Development Ltd. in segments and assembled using barges and the Dutch-built Svanen, the world's largest floating crane. It has 44 spans, main girders that weigh 7,500 tonnes, 310 streetlights, and 7,300 drain ports to allow for water drainage.

ENERGY

THOMAS AHEARN
INVENTOR OF ELECTRIC COOKING OVEN AND MORE

Thomas Ahearn was born in 1855 in the Le Breton Flats part of Ottawa, one of many children of his Irish immigrant parents. He was educated at Ottawa College, but left in his teens to become a telegrapher with the Montreal Telegraph Company in its Chaudière office. After a few years' experience, including working in New York with Western Union Telegraph, Ahearn returned to Ottawa as chief operator for Montreal Telegraph.

Ahearn had a natural skill with inventing and communications, and showed it in 1879 when he copied Alexander Graham Bell's invention of the telephone from an article in *Scientific American* magazine and set up a connection between Ottawa and Pembroke, 177 kilometres away from each other. He was infringing on Bell's patent with his experiment, but it helped him get a job in 1880 when the Bell Telephone company's Ottawa office opened.

In 1881, Ahearn joined with Warren Soper, manager of Dominion Telegraph's office in Ottawa, to set up a company to work on electricity projects. After working on a variety of projects, the company won the contract to develop an electric streetcar system for Ottawa, based on the system developed in Richmond, Virginia. Despite difficulties in finding financing for the new business, Ottawa Electric

Railway was set up in 1891, and eight months later small streetcars were on the road in Ottawa. The cars were heated in the winter by electric heaters, and the tracks cleared by a rotating brush cleaner, both invented by Ahearn. Ahearn's streetcars were sold to twelve major cities across Canada, and in 1948 his company would become the public transit company, O-C Transpo, which is still operating.

Ahearn found another application for his electric heaters, and on August 19, 1892, celebrated his invention of the electric cooking oven with the first meal cooked by electricity at the Ottawa Windsor Hotel. The dinner included eight different meat dishes, vegetables, and pastries. Unfortunately for Ahearn, he sold his patent rights to a company that soon went bankrupt.

Ahearn went on to record other local firsts, such as installing the first streetlights in Ottawa and powering them with hydroelectricity, a system copied in many other Canadian cities. He invented the electric water heater and his original power company, now called Ottawa Hydro, still rents out water heaters as part of its services. Ahearn also gained control of the electric power companies in Hull, establishing a monopoly over the supply of electricity for both cities. And in 1899, Ahearn drove the first electric car in Ottawa.

From 1900 on, Ahearn served in many public roles. He was appointed a director of the Bank of Canada. He was president of nine companies and utilities, and from 1926 to 1932 he served as Chairman of the Ottawa Improvement Commission (now the National Capital Commission). In 1927, he was appointed by Prime Minister Mackenzie King as chair of the Broadcasting Committee for the sixtieth anniversary of Confederation. The Committee oversaw the construction of a network of about 20,000 miles of wire across Canada to make possible the country's first coast-to-coast radio broadcast of the Parliament Hill celebrations on the anniversary.

In 1928, Ahearn had the Champlain bridge across the Ottawa River between Ottawa and Hull built with his own funds. That year, he was appointed to the Privy Council (federal Cabinet), even though he did not hold elected office. He died in Ottawa on June 28, 1938, just after his eighty-third birthday.

BALLARD POWER SYSTEMS
WORLD LEADER IN FUEL CELL TECHNOLOGY

The fuel cell was invented by an American named William Grove in 1839. Internal combustion engines (ICEs), widely used in cars and industrial equipment, operate by burning fuel to create heat, which is then funnelled through pistons or other mechanisms to power the engine. ICEs lose heat as the fuel burns, and also lose power due to friction.

In contrast, fuel cells convert fuel (natural gas, methanol, or hydrogen) directly to electricity-making cells, operating two to three times more efficiently than ICEs. Also unlike ICEs, fuel cells do not burn fuel and therefore do not produce air pollutants. The only by-products of fuel cells are heat and water vapour, which are produced when the fuel is combined with oxygen to produce electricity.

Until Ballard Power Systems of Burnaby, British Columbia, came along, Grove's invention had not been applied. Ballard received extensive government funding when it was starting up in the late 1980s and then raised capital in the stock market in 1993. It has recorded many firsts in fuel cell technology with its proton exchange membrane (PEM) hydrogen fuel cell. To date, however, no vehicles using the system have been commercially produced.

In 1993, Ballard converted the first vehicle to be powered by a fuel cell, an airport shuttle bus. In 1995, it made the first fuel cell to meet the U.S. auto industry standard for motors of 1,000 watts of power per litre, and it was used in the first fuel cell-powered light transit vehicle. In 1997, Ballard produced the first 250-kilowatt fuel cell power plant using the smallest natural gas reformer in the world, and was awarded the first Grove Medal of Honour that year. And in 1998, the first transit buses powered by fuel cells were put to use in Chicago and Vancouver.

Daimler-Chrysler now owns 20 per cent of Ballard Power Systems, and Ford owns 15 per cent of the company. Working with these companies and others, Ballard's power plants and buses are expected to be mass-produced by 2002, and automobiles are expected to follow

in 2004 if all goes well. In the spring of 1999, the Californian government announced that it planned to launch a two-year test program of
fuel cell technology using ten cars and five buses. If the test program
is successful, it will be expanded in 2001 to forty cars and forty buses.
California hopes that its test program and its decree that, by 2003, 10
per cent of each company's total car sales in the state must be ZEV
(zero emissions vehicles) will help push the auto industry to adopt
the technology.

COMMUNICATION

As documented in *Canada Firsts*, Canadians recorded many historical firsts in telecommunications, from the first telephone and wireless and radio communications, to the first geostationary communications satellite. As the following achievements show, Canadians have continued to lead the world in this and other communication fields.

DEVELOPMENTS IN FIBRE-OPTIC NETWORKS

Light moves through thin, flexible, lightweight tubes (or fibres) of glass and carries signals for thousands of kilometres, signals that can be heard at the other end as a voice on a telephone, or converted and printed out on paper through fax machines, or received by computers as text or graphic images. It sounds like fantasy, but this means of communication, called fibre optics, dominates the world today.

Dr. Ken Hill, born February 9, 1939, in Guadalajara, Mexico, has spent most of his life in Canada and has played a major role in the development of this technology. Hill's lifelong interest in science, cultivated through his undergraduate and graduate education in electrical engineering at McMaster University in Hamilton, led him to a job at the federal government's Communications Research Centre (CRC) in Ottawa. There, in 1975, he led his colleagues in the development of "fused coupler" technology, which has become a key part of fibre-optic networks. Fused couplers split signals into two controlled paths so that they can be clearly read by whatever equipment is receiving the signal. The technology is now jointly marketed around the world by the CRC and the Toshiba company, whose people worked with Hill and his colleagues on the invention.

In the late 1970s, Hill and his colleagues found that transparent glass fibres became opaque when they shone light through the fibres. Hill discovered that the light created a mirrorlike effect in the fibres so the light reflected in the fibres instead of shining out through the walls of the fibres. Hill called this phenomenon "photosensitivity" and the mirrorlike effect became known as "Hill gratings" (although they were actually based on Bragg gratings, discovered years earlier by Sir Lawrence Bragg of England).

Gratings are essentially different levels of reflective capacity, and Bragg developed them by sending light into crystals and measuring the changes in reflections. When gratings are created in a fibre, they change the reflective characteristics of the fibre. Hill and his colleagues created gratings by sending intense beams of specific types of light into the fibre, thereby "etching" the fibre with the pattern of the grating. The pattern then "guides" other types of light (with various wavelengths, etc.) through the fibre in an accurate and efficient way.

Ten years passed before his discovery had a practical application, when researchers in the U.S. at the United Technology Research Center (UTRC) discovered a way of sending infrared light through the fibres. Following this development, Hill and his colleagues at the CRC came up with a new, more effective technique for manufacturing fibre gratings, called the "phase mask" technique. By 1994, the CRC and the UTRC had negotiated an agreement to license their technology jointly, and many companies around the world have purchased licences.

Fibre gratings as now produced allow several light beams, each moving at a different speed (or wavelength) to be sent through a single glass fibre, thereby greatly increasing the capacity of each fibre to transmit signals. This process is called "wavelength division multi-plexing." The development of the gratings has been hailed as one of the most important of the tens of thousands of inventions and developments in the fibre-optics industry.

In 1995, in recognition of his discovery of photosensitivity and other technological innovations in fibre optics, Hill won the $100,000 Manning Principal Award, awarded annually since 1982 by the Ernest C. Manning Awards Foundation to encourage and support innovation and enterprise in Canada.

C ANCOM (CANADIAN SATELLITE COMMUNICATIONS INC.) FIRSTS IN SATELLITE TECHNOLOGY

In a region where darkness reigns nineteen hours a day in winter, where there are only 30,000 to 40,000 inhabitants at any one time spread out across thousands of miles of countryside, staying connected to each other, let alone the rest of Canada, is no small challenge. Canada's north did not see a radio station, and then it was a U.S. military station, until the Second World War. And residents had better access to English news broadcasts from the Soviet Union in the 1950s than they did to the Canadian Broadcasting Corporation (CBC).

The Whitehorse TV station (WHTV) operated hand-to-mouth from the late 1950s on, broadcasting local news, weather, and sports to four hundred subscribers. In 1965, Rolf Hougen, owner of a local department store, extended his earlier involvement in the station by taking it over with the help of several investors. He moved the studio, invested in new equipment, began the costly process of taping and shipping programs from Vancouver north to be rebroadcast (a practice approved by the Canadian Radio-television and Telecommunications Commission [CRTC] but protested by Vancouver stations), and eventually expanded to colour broadcasts over three channels.

Technological barriers prevented further developments at WHTV, until they came up with the idea of using Canada's world-leading and relatively new domestic communications satellite (Anik-1, launched in 1972) to gain direct access to the broadcasts from southern stations (see the story of Anik-1 in *Canada Firsts*). A 1979 feasibility study revealed that it was not only residents of the north who desired improved TV reception, but also people living in smaller communities across the country who suffered similar isolation. In order to finance the development of the service, Canadian Satellite Communications Inc. (Cancom) was created, including representatives from broadcasting companies in Vancouver, Victoria, Edmonton, Hamilton, and Montreal.

After overcoming many regulatory and technological barriers, Cancom launched in December 1981. Financial troubles almost derailed the company early on, but when Cancom went to the stock market in 1983, the four million shares sold at five dollars each provided a solid capital base for the company.

Since then the company has constructed the first scrambled satellite television network in the world featuring Canadian signals in French and English, built the most technologically sophisticated commercial master control centre in North America, and supported aboriginal broadcasting by providing free satellite transmission for five native radio services and a free satellite uplink in Whitehorse for TVNC, the world's first aboriginal television network.

Rolf Hougen's dream of TV service for the north has been more than fulfilled, as WHTV now offers its customers twenty-seven channels in colour, connecting them to the whole country, and to all five U.S. networks. In all, Cancom distributes thirty-five Canadian and U.S. signals to over 2,500 cable systems across North America, and it is involved in efforts to bring direct-to-home satellite television to Canada.

WILLARD BOYLE
INVENTOR OF CHARGE COUPLED DEVICE

Willard Boyle's invention may have an obscure name, but it is one of the most widely used pieces of telecommunications equipment ever developed, and it revolutionized the industry.

Born August 19, 1924, in Amherst, Nova Scotia, Boyle and his family moved to Quebec early in his life. They lived in a log cabin, and Boyle did not go to school until grade nine. However, this late start did not prevent him from going on to obtain a Ph.D. in physics from McGill University in 1950.

In 1953, Boyle secured a job with Bell Laboratories where, beyond inventing the charge coupled device, he also developed several other innovations. In 1962, Boyle and his colleague Don Nelson invented the first continuously operating ruby laser, and he obtained the first patent jointly with David Thomas for the semiconductor injection laser (the word "laser" stands for "light amplification by stimulated emission of radiation").

Boyle also contributed to the development of integrated circuits. Integrated circuits are small computer chips that replace several parts of an electrical circuit, thereby reducing the size of any piece of electrical equipment. As a result, they have played an essential role in the development of the telecommunications and electronics industries.

In 1969, Boyle and his colleague George Smith invented the charge coupled device (CCD). As with integrated circuits, the CCD replaced several larger parts of many different types of equipment. The CCD is a light-sensitive grid on a computer chip that captures images, converts them to digital signals, and then transmits them.

CCDs are used in photocopiers and video cameras to capture images, as filters, or to hold images in the memory of a camera. They are also used in the Hubble Space Telescope to capture images of the galaxy. CCDs made possible video cameras that don't use film, as all the images are captured digitally by the CCD and transferred onto computer disk.

Boyle and Smith received the Franklin Institute's Stuart Ballantine Medal in 1973 for their invention. Soon after, Boyle became Executive Director of the Research, Communications Sciences Division at Bell Labs, where he remained until he retired in 1979.

DR. MICHAEL COWPLAND AND TERENCE MATTHEWS
INNOVATIONS IN TELECOMMUNICATION SWITCHES AND GRAPHICS SOFTWARE

Michael Cowpland and Terence Matthews have contributed greatly to the further development of the telecommunications and computer industries in Canada through various companies.

The first development, by Cowpland, came as he was working as manager of circuits design at Microsystems International Ltd. Born on April 23, 1943, in Bexhill, Sussex, England, Cowpland had emigrated to Canada in 1964 to study, and he obtained a master's and a doctorate in engineering at Carleton University, finishing in 1973. His dissertation was on silicon chip design. While studying he was also working, and one of the innovations he came up with was a tone-to-pulse converter to bridge old and new telephone technology. This development greatly aided the transition to new telephone systems.

He and Matthews, a colleague at Microsystems International, left the company to start up Mitel Corporation, which specialized in switches that linked phone lines. The company grew quickly from 1973 to 1982, up to 5,000 employees and $250 million annual sales as one of the world's largest producers of the specialized switches. However, loss of customers and technical problems over the next two years caused problems as company debt increased, and in 1984 Cowpland left the company to new management.

Terence Matthews also left the company, and started up Newbridge Networks Corporation in 1986, a data networking company based in Kanata, Ontario. Under his leadership, Newbridge Networks has become the world's top maker of specialized switches for high-speed multimedia transmissions over telephone and data networks. Many of the largest telecommunications companies in over one hundred countries around the world, including AT&T, GTE Wireless, and Swiss Telecom, use Newbridge's switches. Newbridge employs 6,000 people, and had revenue in 1998 of $1.6 billion. Over the past two years, Matthews has established sixteen Newbridge affiliates, each one specializing in technology that complements Newbridge's network technology, in the hopes that the company will remain at the leading edge of developments in this growing industry.

In 1986, Cowpland formed Corel Corporation (Corel is an acronym for Cowpland Research Labs) to focus on high-tech productivity and multimedia software. By 1989, Corel produced CorelDraw, one of the first software applications for Microsoft's then-new Windows operating system. CorelDraw soon became the number-one-selling PC graphics program, and as of June 1999, it still holds the largest market share with 67.6 per cent of the PC graphics market.

Technical problems again plagued Cowpland's company in 1995, but despite the losses Cowpland invested in purchasing the rights to develop Wordperfect software. An update of the word-processing program combined with other office software and released in 1996 captured a majority of the individual computer user market (it now has the second-largest market share). Corporate and government sales have been more difficult, as many already use Microsoft products and are reluctant to switch. Reluctant to the point of refusal, as Corel found out in 1998 when it submitted a losing bid on a software contract put out by Revenue Canada. In late April 1999, the Federal Court of Appeal ruled that Revenue Canada had not given Corel a fair chance in the bid, in part because the government department already used Microsoft products. Corel lost a similar case in 1996 against the Department of National Defence.

In 1997, Corel became the first company to produce a group of office software using Java script, a computer language that is designed to be used on almost any computer (see "Dr. James Gosling – Inventor of Java computer language" below). Cowpland and the heads of other companies are hopeful that Java could break Microsoft's hold, through the Windows operating system, on the software market. Because it can run on various operating systems, software using Java does not need Windows to run properly, allowing for greater competition in the software market.

By 1999, Corel shipped its products in over seventeen languages, and designed for most computing platforms, to over seventy countries.

THE V-CHIP
A NEW TV "SCREEN"

Research in the late 1980s began to affirm a relationship between violent images broadcast over television and rising rates of violent crime. This relationship, in combination with parents' concerns about their children seeing sexual content and hearing profanity on TV, brought the issue of regulating content on TV to the fore of public consciousness. At the time, Canada and the U.S. had regulations governing what could be shown on TV but it was difficult to monitor individual shows because of the highly diverse audience that television reached.

On December 6, 1989, Tim Collings, an electrical engineering professor at Simon Fraser University in British Columbia, watched the news of the massacre of fourteen women by Marc Lepine at l'École Polytechnique in Montreal, and heard follow-up reports about how viewing violence on TV and in videos could have affected Lepine's mental state. He began to think about how a consumer-driven system could work to regulate what was shown in the home. He came up with the V-chip (V for "viewer"), an electronic box, set atop the TV set, and wired into the TV, to decode information about the content of each show broadcast by the cable networks. The V-chip system allows viewers to choose and block specific programs from being viewed on their televisions.

Beginning in 1990, and with the encouragement of the CRTC, Collings developed the system. In 1996, he was awarded the Manning Principal Award. That year, Collings joined an established company, Tri-Vision International in Toronto, granting the company the exclusive rights for twenty years to license his invention to manufacturers around the world.

Canadian cable companies were required by the CRTC to make the TV-set-top V-chip boxes publicly available as of September 1997. In March 1998, the U.S. Federal Communications Commission required manufacturers to have the V-chip installed in half of all new televisions that are above a certain size by July 1, 1999, and in the other half by January 1, 2000.

DR. JAMES GOSLING
INVENTOR OF JAVA COMPUTER LANGUAGE

James Gosling was born May 19, 1955, and grew up on a farm near Calgary, Alberta. Gosling always had an interest in building stuff, and fiddling with electronics, but his true calling was revealed at age fourteen when he heard about the computer mainframe at the University of Calgary. He learned the combinations to the door locks, and for the next eighteen months let himself in whenever he wanted to work on the computers there. He was such a fixture at the computer laboratory, and already so skilled, that the university hired him to write software for a project. Despite missing many classes, he graduated from high school. He went on to graduate with his Bachelor of Science from the University of Calgary, and then travelled to Carnegie Mellon University to pursue a Ph.D.

Now Dr. Gosling, he joined the company Unix as an engineer, becoming well-known for building the original "Emacs" text editor software. In 1984, Gosling joined Sun Microsystems and worked on several software projects. He and other software developers noted that there was a rapid development of small microprocessors being used in all types of devices from cars to microwave ovens, but there was no ability for all these devices to communicate with each other. This led Gosling to begin in the early 1990s to develop a universal programming language, originally called "Oak." This programming language, which was renamed "Java," could be used with any platform (for example, OS, Unix, or Windows).

At first, Gosling developed a "virtual machine" that would allow his software to run on any operating system, essentially giving away the software. When low-bandwidth on-line networks were set up in the U.S. (forerunners of the World Wide Web, or Internet) the opportunity had arrived to launch Java. Java runs inside Internet browser programs, thereby allowing different computers and microprocessors to talk to each other and draw information from different Internet servers, even servers using different platforms.

As the use of Java spreads, Sun Microsystems faces challenges in keeping the language truly universal, and neutral, in its many applications. Pressure from companies that control specific platforms, especially Microsoft's Windows, has led to Sun working more on applications for these platforms than for others. As with the world's spoken languages, the ease of use of any computer language is not the main factor in how widely it is used, as power, politics, and culture often determine what people hear, and speak.

RADARSAT
WORLD'S MOST POWERFUL COMMERCIAL EARTH OBSERVATION SATELLITE

Canada not only led the world in launching the first domestic geostationary communications satellite, Anik-1, in 1972, but has gone on to other satellite firsts (see "Cancom," above, and story about Anik-1 in *Canada Firsts*). Satellite communication networks are now used to transport TV signals, newspaper content for printing in different locations, and myriad other information.

One major use of satellites is to collect and transmit pictures of the Earth, to track weather patterns, for navigation purposes, and, of course, for spying on other countries and people. RADARSAT, Canada's observation satellite, was originally conceived as a navigational aid for oil tankers forced to travel through the Arctic's icy waters in response to the oil embargo of the early 1970s.

However, by the time of its launch in conjunction with the U.S. National Aeronautics and Space Administration (NASA) in November 1995, RADARSAT was considered the world's most powerful commercial Earth observation satellite. Financed with $500 million from the federal government's Canadian Space Agency, along with $57 million from four provinces (British Columbia, Ontario, Quebec, and Saskatchewan) and $63 million from nine private companies,

RADARSAT was developed by about one hundred Canadian and international organizations.

RADARSAT was the first operational space-borne Synthetic Aperture Radar (SAR). SAR is a microwave instrument which sends pulsing signals to Earth and senses signals received back from Earth. In contrast to optical satellites, which take pictures of the Earth, the signals processed by SAR can produce high-quality images of the Earth in any weather, and through a microwave illumination system it can also produce images during the day or night. RADARSAT can record images of the Earth in blocks 35 to 500 kilometres wide, and pick out objects only 10 metres across in size.

The 3.2-tonne RADARSAT, travelling more than 25,000 kilometres an hour in an 800-kilometre-high orbit, provided the first daily coverage of the entire Arctic region by any satellite. Orbiting the Earth in a pattern fourteen times a day, RADARSAT collects an image of every part of Canada every three days, and every part of the world every five to six days.

The first RADARSAT had a planned lifespan of five years, so in early 1999 RADARSAT had plans to launch a new satellite, able to produce images of objects only three metres by three metres in size. However, U.S. law prohibits anyone from taking pictures of U.S. soil with a resolution more detailed than five by five metres. As a result, and especially because RADARSAT sells its images to anyone (for about $5,000 each), NASA refused to launch the new satellite. Canada will have to negotiate with Britain, France, or Japan to get the satellite launched. NASA was going to pay for the launch in exchange for access to images collected by RADARSAT-2, so Canada now faces an extra cost of about $70 million to get the satellite launched.

JIM CAVERS
INVENTOR OF ADAPTIVE DIGITAL PREDISTORTER (ADP)

Cellular or wireless signals are sent on specific radiowave frequencies (or channels). In order for cellular companies to cope with increased demand for pagers, they employed special high-capacity radio modulators to distinguish signals from each other, allowing for more signals on each radio channel. However, the signals must be boosted by amplifiers to reach transmission towers spread many kilometres apart, and the amplifiers distort the signals, thereby causing interference with other radio channels, which in turn means fewer channels can be used. As a result, the benefit of the modulators was cancelled out by the distortion caused by the amplifiers.

Jim Cavers, an engineering science professor at Simon Fraser University, figured out a solution to this problem in the early 1990s. Called the Adaptive Digital Predistorter (ADP), the device uses a process called linearization. The ADP eliminates amplifier distortion by distorting the signal in exactly the opposite way the amplifier does so that the signal is transmitted correctly. ADPs are installed at the base station of wireless communication systems and connect directly to the power amplifier. Cavers's invention means that distortion is eliminated and more information can be carried per channel and more channels can be used without interference with other channels.

In 1995, Jim Cavers won the B.C. Science and Engineering Gold Medal in recognition of his work with cellular signals. He also won a Manning Principal Award in 1998 for his invention. Cavers licensed his invention to Vancouver-based Glenayre Technologies, which has sold over $30 million in products based on the technology. It is expected that cellular phone companies will soon use ADPs, as demand for cell phones increases.

Cavers also developed a modem for in-flight operations, and it is now used by 70 per cent of commercial aircraft in North America. Called the Aircraft Communication And Reporting System (ACARS), the modem automatically provides weather, engine conditions, estimated-time-of-arrival, and other data to the plane, again without signals getting crossed.

SCHOOLNET
FIRST IN THE WORLD TO LINK PUBLIC SCHOOLS ON-LINE

SchoolNet, a partnership of Canadian and First Nations governments, thirteen telecommunications companies, twelve educational associations, and eighteen technology organizations and associations, was established in 1993 to promote information technology in education. Since then, the program has successfully linked every public school in Canada to the so-called computerized "information highway," making Canada the first country in the world to accomplish this goal.

SchoolNet offers more than one thousand free on-line learning services and projects to the schools, educators, students, and anyone else who connects to its Web site. The program also conducts ongoing research and training in using information technology in the classroom. One component of SchoolNet is Computers for Schools, which operates forty-two computer service centres across Canada and has delivered over 125,000 refurbished computers, along with software, to schools. In addition, more than twenty countries have approached SchoolNet for help with setting up similar networks, and over fifteen agreements have been signed to provide services to these countries.

Although the federal government and others claim that the use of information technology in teaching is crucial in determining Canada's economic and social success in the future, some commentators and studies have concluded that the technology actually hinders learning of fundamental skills such as reading and writing.

While all schools are connected to the information highway through SchoolNet, many schools do not have computers in every classroom. As a result, access to the Internet is severely limited in many schools, often those in smaller, economically disadvantaged communities. SchoolNet's next goal is to extend the connections to the information highway to every public school classroom by March 31, 2001.

MEDICINE

DANIEL DAVID PALMER
WORLD'S FIRST CHIROPRACTOR

In 1865, in Davenport, Iowa, Daniel David Palmer straightened a bump on the spine of a janitor. Immediately afterwards, the janitor regained his lost sense of hearing. Only twenty years old, and originally from Port Perry, Ontario, Palmer was a charismatic healer in Iowa at the time of this event. After Palmer's almost accidental discovery of chiropractic treatment, he began to explore manipulation of the spine to solve other health problems, and to teach his theories and practices.

Chiropractors use no invasive methods in their treatment, which is based on the assumption that good health requires a properly functioning nervous system, beginning with the brain and including the spine. Chiropractors believe that a slight spinal biochemical dysfunction may result in poor health, even in areas not directly associated with the spine. Specific manipulation of certain portions of the spine can relieve many problems. Many medical doctors dismiss this theory, but do concede that certain manipulations do help some patients, and many patients have found relief not available through traditional medicine.

Following in his father's footsteps, B. J. Palmer established the Palmer College of Chiropractic, and continued to research and develop new techniques.

DISCOVERIES AND INVENTIONS CONCERNING THE HUMAN HEART

Over the past century, Canadians and scientists working in Canada have played a leading role in mapping, surgically supporting, exploring, and possibly replacing that most important of organs, the human heart.

MAUDE ABBOTT – MAPPED DISEASES OF THE HEART

Maude Abbott was born March 18, 1869, in St. Andrew's East, Quebec. She won a scholarship to McGill University in Montreal after high school. Upon finishing her undergraduate studies, Abbott planned to study medicine. She wanted to continue at McGill, but at the time women were prohibited from studying medicine there. Instead, Abbott attended Bishop's College in Sherbrooke, Quebec, and studied abroad, becoming a doctor in 1894.

She was hired to work in McGill's pathology department, and wrote a paper on heart murmurs, though a male friend had to present it to the Montreal medical society for her because women were not allowed in the society. In 1898, Abbott became the curator at McGill's Medical Museum and began to catalogue the hearts of people who had died of cardiac problems, as well as to search historical records.

At the time, doctors did not believe that they could operate on the human heart. Over the next few decades, Abbott continued her research, and became Chief of Pathology at a woman's medical college in Pennsylvania in 1923. She returned to McGill in 1926, and pioneered the use of museum exhibits as teaching aids.

With the publication of her catalogue in 1936 as the *Atlas of Congenital Cardiac Disease*, Abbott laid the foundation for modern heart surgery and became known around the world. Despite her achievements, Abbott was never promoted higher than assistant professor at McGill, although she was awarded an honorary medical degree. She was also made an honorary member of the all-male Osler

Society, named after Sir William Osler (who has been called "the most influential physician in history" as detailed in *Canada Firsts*).

On September 2, 1940, Abbott suffered a cerebral hemorrhage and died.

DR. JOHN HOPPS – INVENTOR OF THE CARDIAC PACEMAKER

The story of the pacemaker illustrates how scientific research often produces unintended and significant results, in this case one of the major medical breakthroughs of this century.

In 1949, Dr. Wilfred Bigelow and Dr. J. C. Callaghan were researching hypothermia at the Cardiovascular Laboratory, at the Banting Institute in Toronto. Supported by the National Research Council (NRC) in Ottawa, Dr. John Hopps travelled back and forth to the Banting Institute to help with the research.

John Hopps was born in Winnipeg in 1919, and was educated there through to graduation in engineering from the University of Manitoba in 1941. He then joined the NRC, eventually working in the Electrical Engineering Division. When he joined Bigelow and Callaghan in Toronto, they were examining how cold temperatures slowed the human heart rate. The team noted that when massage or electrical charges were applied to a test animal's heart that had stopped after being cooled it could begin beating again. This led to the idea of creating a device that could start a stopped heart and regulate heart rate.

With his expertise in electrical engineering, Hopps developed what came to be known as the pacemaker. The device would fire a single electrical pulse at appropriate rates to control a heart at normal to lower body temperature and return a fibrillating heart to a normal rate. The first pacemaker was the size of a kitchen table, mainly because batteries at the time were very large.

Hopps's invention was made public in October 1950 at the annual congress of the American College of Surgeons in Boston. Within eight years, with the development of transistors and more efficient batteries, the pacemaker was small enough to be implanted in humans, which first occurred in 1958 in Stockholm, Sweden. The pacemaker was thirty centimetres long and fitted with a NRC-designed circuit that supplied a gentle electric current to the heart muscle without causing injury.

In 1976, Hopps received a Doctorate of Science from the University of Manitoba in recognition of his invention and his service to the profession of engineering. He retired in 1979, and put his invention to good use when he had a pacemaker implanted in himself to correct his sometimes faltering heartbeat. That year he also received the A. G. L. McNaughton gold medal for achievement from the Institute of Electrical and Electronics Engineering. In 1986, Hopps was made a member of the Order of Canada in recognition of his scientific contributions.

In July 1997, Hopps's pacemaker was replaced thirteen years after it had been implanted, because its batteries were failing. When pacemakers were first developed, batteries only lasted six months. Now about 50,000 North Americans, and of course many more people around the world, have pacemakers implanted each year. In November 1998, Hopps died at Ottawa's Civic Hospital.

DR. ADOLFO J. DE BOLD – DISCOVERED THAT THE HEART PRODUCES HORMONES

Born in Paran, Argentina, Adolfo J. de Bold came to Canada in 1968 as a graduate student in the Department of Pathology at Queen's University in Kingston, Ontario. There he obtained his master's and doctoral degrees in pathology, and in 1973 became an assistant professor in the department.

Some of his studies focused on the heart muscle cell, and in 1980 de Bold discovered the Atrial Natriuretic Factor (ANF), a polypeptide hormone produced by the cardiac muscle cell of the heart atrium. His research yielded the first evidence that the heart produces hormones, which surprised many scientists.

For his discovery, Dr. de Bold has been honoured with the Gairdner Foundation International Award, The Ernest C. Manning Principal

Award, and the CIBA Award in Hypertension Research, among other prizes. He is also a Nobel Prize nominee. Dr. de Bold is now a professor of pathology and physiology at the University of Ottawa, and Director of the Cardiac Cell and Molecular Biology Laboratory at the University of Ottawa Heart Institute.

RAY CHU-JENG CHIU – DEVELOPED PROCESS FOR
USING OTHER MUSCLES TO SUPPORT HEART

While John Hopps supported the heart with a pacemaker, developments in research into the heart led to new ways of supporting failing hearts that incorporated pacemaker technology. Ray Chu-Jeng Chiu developed one of these methods.

Born March 13, 1934, in Tokyo, Japan, Chiu received his medical degree from the National Taiwan University, and then emigrated to Canada and obtained his Ph.D. in experimental surgery from McGill University in 1970. The method he developed involves the removal of part of the back muscle of a heart patient, and attaching it to the ribs and wrapping it around the heart. By installing a specially designed pacemaker, the muscle is contracted at the same time as the heart, thereby supporting the heart's function.

The main barrier to this innovation, which Chiu was the first to overcome, is that the heart is the only muscle in the human body that contracts over and over without tiring. With the help of David Inuzzo, a biochemist of York University, Chiu made the back muscle function like the heart muscle by stimulating it electrically at a constant low frequency for four to six weeks. Scientists had discovered in the late 1960s that the electrical stimulation actually alters specific genes in the muscle cells, and Chiu found that the stimulation transformed the back muscle so that it could contract consistently without tiring.

Chiu is now a professor and cardiovascular and thoracic surgeon at the Montreal General Hospital Research Institute.

DR. TOFY MUSSIVAND – INVENTOR OF ARTIFICIAL HEART

Dr. Tofy Mussivand, born in Turkey in 1944 of Kurdish parents, came to Canada in 1965. He has added another chapter to the story of Canadian contributions to heart health. Mussivand's invention, an artificial human heart, will, if all goes well, be implanted in many people over the next several years.

Mussivand's early education and training was in engineering, and when he came to Canada he worked with the Alberta government for fourteen years. He then returned to school, obtaining his Ph.D. in biomedical engineering and medical sciences from the University of Akron and Northwestern Ohio Universities College of Medicine in 1983. From there, he began to explore medical devices and artificial hearts, and for three years was Director of Technical Services for the Cleveland Clinic Foundation, where he saw an artificial heart for the first time. The "heart," however, was a 660-kilogram steel cabinet on wheels that was hooked up to the patient.

Dr. Mussivand was asked by researchers at the clinic to review the barriers to developing an artificial heart that could be implanted in the human body. Out of his review, Mussivand developed criteria for the design of an Electrohydraulic Ventricular Assist Device (EVAD) that could be manufactured at a reasonable cost, be implanted, and be powered and monitored remotely. His conclusions overcame problems that $400 million in research had failed to solve.

Dr. Mussivand returned to Canada in 1989 to head the Ottawa Heart Institute's (OHI) artificial heart team and to chair the Surgical and Engineering Committee. Since 1991, Dr. Mussivand has held the position of Director, Cardiovascular Devices Division at the Institute. He and colleagues at the Institute took his design criteria and developed the first functional EVAD. In 1996, the World Heart Corporation, of which Dr. Mussivand is President and Chief Operating Officer, was started up with the exclusive licence to produce EVAD, which has been renamed the HeartSaver VAD. The World Heart Corporation is developing the HeartSaver VAD for sale worldwide.

The HeartSaver VAD supports blood circulation for people with failing hearts, and it is small enough to be implanted alongside a person's heart without interfering with other organs. It is powered by a patented system, also developed by the Cardiovascular Devices Division at the OHI. The HeartSaver VAD is presently in pre-clinical trials with animals, and if approved by Health Canada, the first human clinical trials are expected in late 1999. If these trials are successful, people with a HeartSaver VAD implant will be able to live a relatively normal, active life, and be monitored from remote locations.

In 1992, Dr. Mussivand also founded the Medical Devices Evaluation Network, an international network of 164 members, which was created to assist in the development and evaluation of medical devices for industry, hospitals, governments, users, and patients. He has published over two hundred scientific publications and chaired over one hundred scientific seminars. He continues to teach at the Carleton University and at the University of Ottawa, and is also on staff at the Ottawa Civic Hospital.

DAVID H. HUBEL
NOBEL PRIZE FOR DISCOVERIES IN HOW VISION WORKS

David Hubel was born in 1926 in Windsor, Ontario, and grew up in Montreal. He attributes his interest in science to his father, who answered his innumerable questions. After completing high school studies at the Strathcona Academy in Outremont, and an undergraduate degree in mathematics and physics at McGill University, Hubel entered medical school at McGill.

He became fascinated with the nervous system, spending his summers at the Montreal Neurological Institute, and spending two of his three years of post-graduation hospital training in neurology. Then, in 1954, Hubel spent a year at Johns Hopkins University in the U.S. in neurology. Because his parents were both born in the U.S., Hubel also held American citizenship, and as a result he was drafted by the army while in the U.S. He was assigned to the Neuropsychiatry Division of the Walter Reed Army Institute of Research.

While at Walter Reed, Hubel began his research into vision. In 1958, he moved to another laboratory at the Wilmer Institute at Johns

Hopkins, and then with that laboratory team to the Harvard Medical School in Boston the following year. There he began to collaborate with Torsten Wiesel of Sweden in a twenty-year exploration of information-processing by the visual system.

Hubel and Wiesel tapped nerve-cell impulses in the various layers of the visual cortex of the brain, and found that the message or image reaching the brain from the eyes is interpreted with respect to its contrasts, linear patterns, and the movement of the image across the retina of the eye. One nerve cell after another provides specific details of the image, and in a sequence the image is put together and then stored in memory. They also found that the cells doing the interpreting are arranged in columns, each about two by two millimetres, and each column interprets a similarly sized area of the image. As a result of their work, the visual cortex is the best understood part of the brain.

Another interesting discovery the two made was that the brain's ability to interpret images is developed right after birth, so any distortions or impairments in a newborn baby's vision can affect his or her ability to see for the rest of his or her life.

For their breakthroughs in research into the ability of the brain to interpret the code of the images sent from the eyes, Hubel and Wiesel were awarded half of the 1981 Nobel Prize in Medicine, sharing it with American Roger W. Sperry, who discovered functions of various hemispheres of the brain.

DR. KEITH INGOLD
WORLD LEADER IN CHEMISTRY OF ORGANIC FREE RADICALS

What comes to mind when you hear the words "organic free radicals" – revolutionary people challenging the system? A give-away of radical chic clothing? A new organic vegetable? Actually, free radicals are atomic particles that react in a particular way to chemical changes, in many cases causing oxidation. The oxidation caused by free radicals can cause disease in humans, spoil food, and slow the flow of automobile oils, making them useless for lubricating engines.

Keith Ingold has diagnosed many of the effects of free radicals, and in doing so has convinced a sceptical scientific community of their importance in causing disease. Born in England in 1929, Ingold did an undergraduate degree in chemistry at the University of London, and his Doctorate of Philosophy in Chemistry at Oxford University. He emigrated to Canada in 1951 to do postdoctoral research in Ottawa at the National Research Council (NRC). At that time, only two Canadian universities offered doctoral degrees in chemistry.

In the 1960s, Ingold and his colleagues at the NRC began to document the rates of free radical chemical reactions, leading the world in this area. His team was the first to define the stability and persistence of free radicals, and also led the world in studies of anti-oxidants, chemicals that trap and neutralize free radicals, thereby preventing their damaging effects. Initially, their research focused on the effects of free radicals on engine oils, and led to the development of much more effective lubricating oils for automobiles that contain phenols as anti-oxidants.

In the 1980s, Ingold undertook pioneering research that proved that vitamin E was an effective anti-oxidant for humans. Unlike most scientists at the time, Ingold believed that vitamin E must be an anti-oxidant because it is a phenol. Ingold, with his colleagues, also determined through a series of trials, including experimenting on himself in one case, the best ways to deliver vitamin E to the human body. His findings provoked new thinking on links between vitamin deficiencies, vitamin supplements, and human health, and ongoing research has since identified several vitamins that protect cells from free radicals and help prevent or slow the onset of diseases such as strokes, cancer, heart attacks, and arthritis.

Dr. Ingold has authored more than 450 scientific articles, and for his work has been awarded honorary degrees from six universities, along with the Henry Marshall Tory Medal of the Royal Society of Canada, the Izaak Walton Killam Memorial Prize of the Canada Council, the Chemical Institute of Canada's Medal, and the Linus Pauling Award from the American Chemical Society. He has also been appointed to the Order of Canada, and elected a Fellow of the

Royal Society of Canada, the Chemical Institute of Canada, and the Royal Society of London. In 1998, he was awarded the Canada Gold Medal for Science and Engineering by the National Sciences and Engineering Research Council of Canada (NSERC).

Dr. Ingold works in the Steacie Institute for Molecular Sciences at the NRC in Ottawa, and he is also an adjunct professor at Carleton University.

DR. KELVIN OGILVIE
INVENTOR OF THE "GENE MACHINE" AND FIRST TO SYNTHESIZE RNA

Before 1980, it took scientists months to synthesize DNA. DNA, or deoxyribonucleic acid, is a molecular material that nearly all living organisms contain, and it carries information about the genetic tendencies of each organism. Delays in producing synthetic DNA meant delays in researching many theories about exactly how DNA works.

Canadian Dr. Kevin Ogilvie solved this problem. Born in Summerville, Nova Scotia, on November 6, 1942, Ogilvie graduated with a science degree from Acadia University in 1964, and then obtained his Ph.D. at Northwestern University in 1968.

A long-term interest in the area, and key financial support provided by the federal government's National Sciences and Engineering Research Council of Canada (NSERC), helped Ogilvie invent the automated gene synthesizer, or "gene machine.". The gene machine can build DNA sequences in a matter of hours rather than months, and it has been widely used in laboratories since its creation.

The process for synthesizing DNA was discovered in 1968, but it was not until 1988 that the process for synthesizing RNA was discovered, also by Ogilvie. RNA, or ribonucleic acid, is a molecule that builds proteins in cells, essentially following the genetic instructions contained in DNA. After the equivalent of two hundred person-years of research, the team headed by Ogilvie at McGill University was able to create a protective material that allowed RNA to be synthesized without breaking down. The development of synthetic RNA has increased the understanding of how cells operate, which has increased the possibility of cures for various diseases.

For example, synthetic RNA, now created regularly by Ogilvie 's "gene machine," can be used in drugs to attack viruses made of RNA, such as the retroviruses leukemia and AIDS. As Ogilvie explains it: "You look at the retrovirus, find a sequence of its RNA that is important to its functioning, then make a piece that is an exact complement, but backwards. It will attach itself to the viral RNA and destroy its ability to replicate."

Ogilvie also developed the drug Glanciclovir, which fights the cytomegalovirus or CMV. For his work, Ogilvie won the Manning Principal Award in 1992. He is currently a professor of chemistry at Acadia University.

DR. TAK MAK
LED THE DISCOVERY OF CANCER-RELATED GENES

Genes are not unlike genies. Difficult to pin down and almost magical, they are found in human bodies and play key roles in our day-to-day lives. For example, the genes in our immune system protect us from viruses, allergies, and other physical reactions to the world around us.

In 1983, our understanding of our immune system took a huge leap forward with the discovery of the T-cell receptor, a gene and a key component of the system. A team led by University of Toronto professor Tak Mak, senior scientist at the Ontario Cancer Institute/Princess Margaret Hospital, made the discovery. After the discovery, scientists could manipulate the T-cell receptor in tests with animals to discover which genes are involved in diseases such as diabetes and multiple sclerosis, thereby pointing to possible methods of treating these diseases.

Tak Mak was born in China on October 4, 1946. As he grew up he wasn't very good in school, being more interested in soccer, but with a push from his mother he worked hard and succeeded. He studied at the University of Wisconsin, and then went on to do a Ph.D at the University of Alberta in immunology and molecular biology. He began his research at the Ontario Cancer Institute in 1972, and has been senior scientist there since 1974.

Further work over several years by Mak, again leading a team of researchers and with support in part from the federal government's National Cancer Institute of Canada, resulted in the discovery of the function of the PTEN gene in 1998, a year after the gene was first discovered. What Mak's team found was that the PTEN gene blocks the signal scientists call PKB/AKT. Cells continuously receive signals that tell them to live, grow, change, or die. If a cell is damaged, then it is supposed to die, but the PKB/AKT sends a signal to the damaged cell telling it to continue to live. If a cell is missing in the PTEN gene, then the PKB/AKT signal gets through and the damaged cell grows into a tumour.

Knowing the function of the PTEN gene is very important because if a mutation of the PTEN is found in a tumour, then 90 per cent of the chemotherapy drugs usually used in treatment can be ruled out because the drugs will not be able to kill the tumour. Other drugs that may help can then be designed to kill that type of tumour. Also, researchers can look for ways of replacing the PTEN gene in cells that don't have it naturally.

As a result of the work of Mak's team and of others, the Ontario Cancer Institute/Princess Margaret Hospital, a teaching hospital of the University of Toronto, has achieved an international reputation as a leader in cancer research and treatment.

DR. PHILIP SEEMAN
DISCOVERED RECEPTORS THAT CAUSE SCHIZOPHRENIA

When he was a postdoctoral student in 1969, Dr. Philip Seeman began examining the brains of people with schizophrenia for signs of the cause of the illness. However, knowledge of how the brain works was more limited at the time, so no patterns could be determined. Seeman had the idea of testing various effective treatment drugs with the hope of discovering the parts of the brain the drugs affected.

In 1974, working at the University of Toronto, Seeman identified the dopamine D2 receptor as a factor in schizophrenia, along with the D4 receptor. Dopamine plays a role in the brain's message system, and receptors, located on cell walls, are proteins that receive the messages. Seeman discovered the people with schizophrenia had six times as much D4 receptor in their brains. This amount of D4 may overactivate dopamine, thereby overloading the brain of schizo-phrenics with hallucinations and delusional messages.

Between 1988 and 1991, Dr. Seeman, along with his colleagues Dr. Hyman Niznik and Dr. Hubert Van Tol, cloned dopamine receptors D1, D2, D4, and D5. This allowed pharmaceutical companies to develop more effective drugs for treatments, and with fewer side effects. The challenge now is to isolate the gene for the D4 receptor protein, and to determine why it is more abundant and active in the brains of schizophrenics.

In 1994, Dr. Seeman and his colleagues won the Prix Galien, which was created in France to recognize researchers who have made a vital contribution to pharmaceutical research. The prize had been awarded all over Europe, but it was the first time it had been given in Canada.

DR. JIM McEWEN
INVENTOR OF AUTOMATIC TOURNIQUET SYSTEM

According to Dr. Jim McEwen, a biomedical engineer, trying to perform certain surgical procedures without using tourniquets is like trying to repair a watch while immersed in an inkwell. Tourniquets cut off the flow of blood to an area of the body, allowing the surgeon to perform what is called "dry and bloodless surgery."

However, tourniquets are difficult to monitor and have been known to cause nerve damage, blood loss, and even temporary heart stoppage. McEwen had viewed a few cases of similar problems as the Director of Biomedical Engineering at the Vancouver General

Hospital. To prevent these unintended consequences of surgery, McEwen came up with the idea of adding a microprocessor computer to a tourniquet, allowing the surgeon to monitor the patient's blood pressure in the area cut off from the body's blood supply and make adjustments to the tourniquet as necessary throughout the operation.

McEwen obtained a patent in Canada for his Automatic Tourniquet System in 1994, and a U.S. patent in 1995. Versions of his invention are used, according to estimates, in 16,000 operations daily around the world. In 1997, Dr. McEwen won the Manning Principal Award for this innovation in medical technology.

DR. IMANT LAUKS
INVENTOR OF A BETTER BLOOD-TESTING MACHINE

Usually, blood analysis takes hours or even days. The time involved can cause delays, and sometimes critical problems, with the diagnosis of a patient's medical condition. In the mid 1980s, Dr. Imant Lauks set out to lessen the time needed for results by inventing a better blood-testing machine, and luckily for all of us he was successful.

Born in 1952 in Bradford, England, of Latvian immigrant parents, Lauks studied chemistry in his undergraduate years, and then received his doctorate in electrical engineering in 1977 from London University. He obtained a position as professor of electrical engineering at the University of Pennsylvania.

In 1986, Lauks came up with the idea and a hand-drawn design for his blood tester. With his colleagues, he started up i-Stat Canada Ltd. in Kanata, Ontario, and began development of the tester. The i-Stat system they came up with is different from traditional blood testers in that it uses only a few drops of blood instead of several milligrams, and it can complete twelve of the most common blood tests in ninety seconds instead of a few hours. The system can be carried in one hand, and channels the blood samples onto silicon chips containing chemicals that react in specific ways to the blood. The chips transmit through electrical signals the results of the reactions to an analyzer, and then to a display screen. The results can also be entered into computer data networks and stored for easy recall anywhere.

Among its many benefits, the i-Stat system reduces the need for blood transfusions, reduces waiting time in emergency rooms, and allows for monitoring of patients who are being transported. After clinical trials and regulatory approvals, the i-Stat system was first made available in 1992. In 1995, Hewlett-Packard of Palo Alto, California, invested $61 million in i-Stat Canada Ltd. and now markets the i-Stat system around the world.

To date, sales of the i-Stat system have been mainly in the U.S., but the system has been used by NASA and the Russian space station MIR for blood-testing of astronauts in space. The company employs about four hundred people in Kanata, and five hundred people in total, and had 1998 sales of $37 million.

DR. MICHAEL SMITH
NOBEL PRIZE WINNER FOR DISCOVERY OF PROCESS
FOR MUTATING GENES

As described above with regard to the invention of the "gene machine" in 1980 by Dr. Kelvin Ogilvie, DNA is a molecular material that carries information about the genetic tendencies of each organism. Dr. Ogilvie's machine made genetic research much easier by greatly reducing the time needed to synthesize DNA .

Scientists researching causes of defects or mutations in genes still had a problem, however. In order to create study specimens, organisms had to be exposed to radiation or chemicals, which created all sorts of mutations through which the researcher would have to sort and find the specific mutation he or she wished to study. Dr. Michael Smith solved this problem and for his efforts won the Nobel Prize for chemistry in 1993.

Born April 26, 1932, in Blackpool, England, Smith has been living and working in and around Vancouver since 1956, when he went to the University of British Columbia as a postdoctoral student in chemistry. When he arrived in Vancouver, he began working in a laboratory that focused on molecular chemistry, a new area for Smith. Fortunately for the world, his work there led to his eventual discovery of a process to substitute a synthetic strand for one of the two strands of matching nucleotides that make up DNA in any organism. The synthetic strand can be different in many ways from the natural strand and, depending on the difference, can be used to create a variety of mutations.

Researchers can use Smith's technique, called "site-directed mutagenesis," to create DNA with the specific mutation they want to study. Studies of mutations are done to track not only the reasons for the mutations, but also the effects of the mutations. Through repeated testing, which Smith's method makes much easier, researchers can narrow down the causes of mutations, and possible cures.

Dr. Smith also won the Manning Principal Award, in 1995. Admirably, he did not keep the $500,000 he received for his 1993 Nobel Prize. He gave half of the award money to research on the genetics of schizophrenia, and the other half to Science World B.C. and the Society for Canadian Women in Science and Technology.

KARLEE KOSOLOFSKI
SURVIVED LOWEST BODY TEMPERATURE EVER RECORDED

On February 23, 1995, a terrible thing happened to Karlee Kosolofski. Only two years old at the time, she was accidentally locked outside of her house in Regina, Saskatchewan, for six hours when it was -22.2 degrees Celsius (-8 degrees Fahrenheit).

Amazingly, though she suffered frostbite and had to have her left leg amputated above the knee, Karlee survived the lowest body temperature ever recorded, 14.2 degrees Celsius (57.5 degrees Fahrenheit), and made a full recovery.

DISCOVERY OF GENE FOR FAMILIAL ALZHEIMER'S DISEASE

Alzheimer's disease slowly destroys the central nervous system and causes memory loss and decreased ability in reasoning and perception. About 10 per cent of Alzheimer's patients in Canada (30,000 people) suffer from familial Alzheimer's, which is inherited and strikes people between the ages of thirty to sixty. The other 90 per cent that suffer from Alzheimer's are affected after age sixty-five.

In 1985, a team of researchers at the University of Toronto's Centre for Research in Neurodegenerative Diseases (CRND) began to try to find the gene that causes familial Alzheimer's. Eventually they succeeded, in no small part due to the funding support from the Alzheimer's Association of Ontario, private donors such as Mark Tanz (the building that houses the CRND bears his family name), and the federal government's Medical Research Council of Canada.

The team's discovery, announced in June 1995, made news around the world. The discovery was the result of an intriguing genetic investigation. The group began by looking for clues in a family that had a pattern of inheriting the disease. They narrowed the search to part of chromosome 14, but when they examined all the known genes on that chromosome, none could be linked to the disease. They began to examine new genes, and after nineteen tries found a gene with mutations that matched sufferers of Alzheimer's.

From 1992 on, the principal investigator, Peter St. George-Hyslop, a professor of neurology in the Department of Medicine and Director of the CRND, worked with thirty-two other people spread across fourteen institutions from five countries, cloning the gene and then defining the mutations that cause the disease.

Inheriting a disease is a challenging event, and equally challenging is knowing that you will get a disease in the future. Now that testing for familial Alzheimer's is possible, procedures are being set up to ensure that anyone tested receives counselling.

Discovery and Development of Light-Activated Drugs

Just as people's eyes vary in sensitivity, some materials are more sensitive to light than others. A Vancouver company has focused on these materials, and through testing the molecules that make up these materials, has developed drugs that respond to light.

In 1981, Julia Levy, a professor of microbiology at the University of British Columbia (UBC), set up a company with some colleagues called Quadra Logic Technologies (now QLT) to explore the possibility of developing some of their discoveries into products and selling them for profit. Levy, born in Singapore on May 15, 1934, had been interested in biology since she took walks in the woods as a child with her mother near their home. Inspired by her grade eleven biology teacher, Levy obtained her undergraduate degree in microbiology from UBC, and then her Ph.D. at University College in London, England.

Levy and her colleagues struggled at first to develop a marketable product, as many biotechnology companies do. By 1986, the company was trying to create a light-activated drug when Levy heard that the development of a laser-activated drug called Photofrin, initially created by the Roswell Park Cancer Institute in Buffalo, New York, was being shelved by Johnson & Johnson because of the costs of lasers at that time. When they heard of good results from some tests of Photofrin, QLT decided to buy the rights to develop the drug, in partnership with American Cyanamid Inc. of New Jersey.

QLT discovered through clinical trials that when Photofrin was injected into the blood stream it was carried to some cancerous tumours by molecules called lipoproteins. These tumours require lipoproteins to grow, and so absorbed more lipoproteins (and therefore more Photofrin) than healthy cells. A couple of days later a significant amount of the drug would be absorbed by the tumour, and then doctors would focus a red laser beam through the skin directly at the tumour. Because human skin is transparent to red light, the laser light activates the drug, changing it into a molecule called singlet oxygen, which destroys some cancer cells.

There are two problems with Photofrin, however. First, it does not work with all tumours, and many types of cancers cause many different types of tumours. So far it has been approved for use with lung and esophageal cancers in many countries, and also for bladder cancer in Canada. Another complication is that patients receiving treatment with Photofrin must avoid contact with sunlight for six weeks, in order not to overactivate the drug.

Levy had a vision, so to speak, of another drug, which has had very promising results from start to finish in trials. Called Visudyne, this light-activated drug has a positive impact on patients who have a condition that affects the retina of the eye. Called age-related macular degeneration, this condition is the leading cause of blindness in people fifty and over, and affects about 500,000 people worldwide each year. When her mother became blind from the disease, Levy was prompted to search for a treatment.

Although Visudyne has not yet been approved for use, the trial results have been so positive that it is expected to be approved soon. One of the benefits of Visudyne is that it is designed so that its sensitivity to light drops off after twenty-four hours, eliminating the need to avoid sunlight after treatment. QLT is also developing treatments for diseases such as arthritis, psoriasis, and multiple sclerosis, using a new photodynamic drug called BPD.

EDUCATION AND SOCIAL WELFARE

CANADIANS AT THE UNITED NATIONS

Many Canadians have served in various positions at the United Nations along with representatives of the more than 150 member countries of the organization. Some of the notable people responsible for firsts and foremosts in Canada's contributions to the UN are set out below.

JOHN PETERS HUMPHREY – DRAFTER OF THE UNIVERSAL DECLARATION OF HUMAN RIGHTS

John Peters Humphrey, born April 30, 1905, in the town of Hampton, New Brunswick, would go on to write a document of worldwide importance. Humphrey studied law and was called to the Quebec Bar in 1929. For a few years he practised law, and then joined the Faculty of Law at McGill University in 1936, where he worked for a decade.

In 1946, Humphrey was appointed Director of the United Nations Division of Human Rights. The United Nations, an international organization of countries, was created in 1945 to promote international peace, security, and cooperation. Over the next two years, beginning with a draft written by Humphrey, the United Nations considered the Universal Declaration of Human Rights. The Declaration, which has changed the way international law deals with violations of human rights, was adopted on December 10, 1948, as a resolution of the United Nations General Assembly.

For over twenty years, the first draft of the Declaration was attributed to René Cassin, a French jurist and United Nations delegate. When the actual first draft of the Declaration was discovered, it was in Humphrey's own handwriting, and he was given long overdue credit.

Humphrey worked at the UN until 1966, overseeing the implementation of sixty-seven international conventions and the constitutions of dozens of countries before returning to McGill University. He taught at McGill, while continuing to travel widely and represent victims of human rights violations, until his death in 1995. In recognition of the fiftieth anniversary of the Declaration in December 1998, Canada Post issued a stamp bearing a portrait of Humphrey.

Canada also constructed the world's first monument to commemorate human rights in 1988. Designed by well-known Montreal architect Melvin Charney and located in Ottawa, the monument is built out of pink Manitoba granite. Chiseled into the face of the ten-metre-high monument are the first words of the Universal Declaration of Human Rights, "All human beings are born free and equal in dignity and rights."

When the monument was first unveiled by the Dali Lama of Tibet, Prime Minister Brian Mulroney did not go to the opening in order not to offend China, though China has occupied Tibet since the 1940s and has carried out acts of genocide and cultural assassination against the Tibetan people. In September 1998, Nelson Mandela visited the monument and unveiled a plaque that has been attached to the monument in honour of John Peters Humphrey's contribution to human rights protection in the world.

LESTER B. PEARSON – 1957 NOBEL PEACE PRIZE WINNER
Lester B. Pearson, born April 23, 1897, in Newtonbrook, Ontario (now part of Toronto), went on to lead Canada as prime minister, and on an international level at the United Nations. At age sixteen, Pearson

entered the University of Toronto, but his studies were interrupted by Canada's declaration of war in 1914. The University sponsored a hospital unit during the war, and Pearson volunteered with the unit for two years in England, Egypt, and Greece until he was old enough to enlist with the armed forces. He was injured while serving with the Royal Flying Corps, and as a result served as a training instructor for the rest of war. He also continued his studies, graduating in 1919.

After two years working for his uncle's meat processing company, Pearson won a two-year scholarship to Oxford University in England. In 1922, he played with the British ice hockey team at the Olympics, and graduated the following year with a master's in history. He returned to the University of Toronto in 1924 as a professor in the history department, but after four years he left to become first secretary in the federal Department of External Affairs.

Pearson participated in several international conferences over the next seven years, and then moved on to the office of the High Commissioner for Canada in England, serving there until 1941. He returned to External Affairs in Ottawa, and in 1942 was transferred to the ambassador's office in Washington, D.C., where he later served as ambassador, 1945–46. While in Washington, Pearson participated in the establishment of the United Nations and its agencies, the Food and Agricultural Organization and the United Nations Relief and Rehabilitation Administration. In 1946, Pearson returned to External Affairs, and two years later ran successfully for federal Parliament for the Liberal Party, becoming Minister of External Affairs in Prime Minister Louis St. Laurent's cabinet.

Over the next nine years as a Minister, Pearson played a key role in the establishment of the North American Treaty Organization (NATO), headed the Canadian delegation to the UN (serving as president of the UN's General Assembly in 1951–52), and chaired the General Assembly's Special Committee on Palestine. He also proposed a successful resolution to send a UN Emergency Force to police the area of conflict during the Suez Canal conflict in 1956, the first use of an international peacekeeping force.

In 1957, in recognition of his contribution to international policy in the post-Second World War period, and especially for his role in resolving the Suez crisis, Pearson was awarded the Nobel Peace Prize. The Liberals lost the federal election that year, and Pearson became leader of the party in opposition. The Liberals formed a minority government following the 1963 election, and over the next five years Prime Minister Pearson, at the urging of the newly formed New Democratic Party (until 1961 the Co-operative Commonwealth Federation), passed laws setting up old age pensions, the health care system, and financial assistance for education. As a result, he left a legacy, in Canada and around the world, of initiatives for peace and social progress, many of which have, unfortunately, failed to live up to their goals, let alone the ideals underlying them.

MAURICE STRONG – HEADED UN ENVIRONMENTAL AND REFORM INITIATIVES

Maurice Strong served as the first head of the United Nations Environment Program (UNEP) and also chaired a 1992 international conference on environmental issues known as the Rio Earth Summit. The Rio Summit was the largest gathering of heads of state in history. Strong was also appointed by Kofi Annan, the Secretary-General of the UN since 1996, to draft a plan for changes to the UN's structure and activities. The plan was released in 1997.

LOUISE FRÉCHETTE – HIGHEST RANKING WOMAN AT THE UN

Louise Fréchette has played an important role in implementing the UN reform plan since 1998, when she was appointed as the UN's first Deputy Secretary-General, the most senior UN position ever held by a woman. Fréchette, from Montreal, was Canada's ambassador to the UN from 1992 to 1994 and the first Secretary at Canada's permanent mission to the UN in Geneva. As Deputy Secretary-General, Fréchette is overseeing the first phase of changes at the UN, a process of reducing administrative costs and internal conflicts among UN agencies and shifting savings into a fund, called the Development Account, that will be spent on new development projects chosen by representatives of the member countries in the UN General Assembly. The Account is expected to total $300 million by 2002.

LOUISE ARBOUR – CHIEF PROSECUTOR OF UN WAR CRIMES TRIBUNALS

Louise Arbour is another Canadian who reached the top of the UN system, in her case the international justice system. A law professor for thirteen years at Osgoode Hall Law School from 1974 to 1987, and a former Justice of the Ontario Court of Appeal, Arbour was offered the job of Chief Prosecutor for the UN's international war crimes tribunals in former Yugoslavia and Rwanda in 1995 by then UN Secretary-General Boutros Boutros Ghali. Her term began on October 1, 1996. The former Yugoslavia tribunal, set up in May 1993, has indicted more than seventy people and the Rwanda tribunal, set up in November 1994, has indicted over twenty people.

In late May 1999, Arbour indicted Slobodan Milosevic, President of Yugoslavia, for crimes against humanity, the first time an international court had charged a head of state in power of war crimes. On June 10, 1999, Arbour was appointed to the Supreme Court of Canada. As a result, she left her position as war-crimes prosecutor in September 1999, one year before her term finished. A former law clerk for the Supreme Court in 1971–72, Arbour became the third woman on the nine-judge court, replacing retiring Justice Peter Cory.

QUICKLAW
FIRST COMPUTERIZED LEGAL INFORMATION RETRIEVAL SYSTEM

In 1960, Hugh Lawford was in his third year as a professor at the Faculty of Law at Queen's University. He began to work on the Queen's Treaty Project, a computerized registry of international treaties for eighteen Commonwealth countries that had recently become independent. Following this project, Lawford was asked to head up a study of legal information computer systems initiated by Queen's principal John Deutsch.

Called the "Queen's University Investigation of Computing and Law" or "QUIC/LAW" for short, the project was initially a partnership with IBM Canada. However, in 1972, the federal government forced IBM to stop participating in the project, and Queen's also cut funding for the project in 1973. In response, Lawford and Richard von Briesen purchased QUIC/LAW from Queen's, under an agreement that allowed them to get academic credit for work on the project, while they pledged to pay Queen's $100,000 within seven years.

Lawford and von Briesen incorporated as QL Systems Ltd., and continued to develop the system with their own money. They were almost broke when a commercial legal text publisher invested $150,000, allowing the project to continue and become the first computerized legal information retrieval system in the world.

QL Systems' product, now known as QUICKLAW, has continued to expand since then. Subscribers from across the country telephone through their computer modem to QUICKLAW, and then through one of the first on-line and fully searchable text databases ever created, they find laws and judgments from many jurisdictions, as well as business, legal, and news information, with just the push of a few buttons. QUICKLAW earns revenue of more than $10 million a year and controls more than 90 per cent of the market for the service in Canada.

CASEY HOUSE
WORLD'S FIRST AIDS HOSPICE

In 1988, a group of people in Toronto, led by writer and social activist June Callwood, overcame financial, organizational, and many other barriers to set up Casey House, the world's first hospice for people living with AIDS. Casey House Hospice provides holistic care, with nurses, physicians, counsellors, and other staff and volunteers working together to provide around-the-clock physical, psychological, emotional, and spiritual support for thirteen people who live at the House, and also to twenty other people who live in their own homes.

Casey House has been recognized internationally for its innovative approach to care for people with AIDS. The House has provided care to about 10 per cent of the people across Canada reported to have died with AIDS.

C ANADA'S HEALTH CARE SYSTEM
IS IT STILL FOREMOST IN THE WORLD?

As detailed in *Canada Firsts*, Canada's health care system was considered the best in the world. However, doubts have grown that the system is maintaining its number-one position. For example, the Commonwealth Fund conducted a survey in 1998 that showed greater satisfaction with the British health care system than with Canada's.

Canada's health care system is based on five principles that are set out in the Canada Health Act: universal coverage, accessibility, comprehensive benefits, portability of benefits, and public administration. However, cuts in government funding for the system caused mainly by the 1995 federal budget forced drastic compromises in the delivery of services and threatened the system's ability to fulfill its principles, as even the National Forum on Health, a federal government-appointed task force, recognized in its 1997 report.

While the federal government restored some funding to the system in the 1999 budget, much of that financing will likely go to repairing the damage done by the cuts, as opposed to implementing a comprehensive plan for delivering health care more effectively to Canadians. A major part of the problem, the National Forum on Health and others have concluded, is that government officials ignore evidence about how the system is performing when making their decisions, or do not even collect enough information to make good decisions.

It is widely recognized, based on studies of health care systems around the world, that ways of delivering health care services can change without threatening the fulfillment of the principles of Canada's system if those changes involve an emphasis on prevention of disease, reducing unnecessary surgery and ineffective treatments, and offering services at a community level with service providers from many disciplines involved. It is also widely recognized from these studies that the principles will not be fulfilled if private health care providers are allowed to provide services, because the bottom-line profit motive of private companies conflicts directly with providing services universally, accessibly, and comprehensively. As in many areas of business, Canada faces great pressure from private U.S. companies who want to provide health care services to Canadians.

As detailed in *Canada Firsts*, the abandonment of Canada's drug patent system in 1987 that had ensured the availability of inexpensive, generic versions of pharmaceutical drugs was an earlier undermining of Canada's health care system that also benefitted private companies at the expense of the public interest. Unfortunately, the cuts in government funding imposed in the 1995 federal budget were so quick and deep that they have further opened up opportunities for private health care providers to play a greater role in Canada's system. To reverse these damaging developments, the National Forum on Health and many others have called for the expansion of Canada's health care system to cover home care services and pharmaceutical drug costs.

CALGARY GENERAL HOSPITAL – WORLD'S LARGEST DEMOLITION

The demolition of the Calgary General Hospital on October 4, 1998, is perhaps the greatest symbol of how the 1995 cuts and the lack of evidence-based decision-making have undermined Canada's health care system. The hospital was closed as a result of health care cuts by the Alberta government, but some observers estimate that a new hospital will have to be built within the decade to meet health care needs for the city. The demolition of the hospital set the world record for most buildings ever demolished at one time. Engineered by the U.S. company Demolition Inc. of Idaho, seven buildings ranging from four storeys to ten storeys high were demolished using 1,880 kilograms of explosives, six kilometres of wire, and 5,744 blasting caps.

The total cost of the demolition and clean-up was $8.5 million, and very little of the material could be salvaged because it was damaged. A local charity raised money by selling 3,000 bricks that could be salvaged as souvenirs for $3.00 each, and other salvaged bricks were used to build a memorial on the site dedicated to the hospital.

CANADA'S ANTI-SMOKING CAMPAIGN
MORE WORLD FIRSTS, MORE TO DO

As detailed in *Canada Firsts*, Canada's anti-smoking campaign led the world in the early nineties in many areas. Since then, Canada has registered other world firsts in its campaign, while taking some steps backwards.

First of all, Air Canada extended its ban on smoking on domestic flights to international flights that depart from Canada. This measure was expected to cause a drop in passengers, but levels actually increased. As a result, U.S. airlines and other nations' airlines that initially opposed the ban have followed Canada's lead.

Under a new law in British Columbia, Imperial Tobacco of Montreal became the first company in the world, on October 30, 1998, to publish a list of the levels of forty separate toxic substances present in cigarettes. Tobacco companies have been one of the few manufacturing sectors that have not been required to disclose the ingredients of their products. Other governments are following B.C.'s lead in legislating ingredients disclosure, such as member states of the European Union, Thailand, and the State of Massachusetts.

In September 1994, Canada became the first country to require by law an increase in the size of health warning labels on tobacco packages, from a small warning on the side of the package to a label that takes up 20 per cent of the front and back of the package. The labels must be black on white or white on black. Australia, South Africa, Singapore, Thailand, and Poland have since introduced similar requirements. Canada is now moving towards increasing the size of the warning even further.

In addition, the federal government reduced taxes on tobacco drastically in a move to decrease smuggling of cigarettes from U.S. border states into Canada. However, it has become clear that Canada's target should have been the tobacco companies, not tobacco taxes. Before the reduction in tobacco taxes, Canadian tobacco companies increased exports of cigarettes to U.S. border states knowing that it would facilitate increased smuggling. In early 1999, U.S. police forces arrested a senior executive of the R. J. Reynolds Company on smuggling-related charges, and the executive is now awaiting trial. In addition, the cut in tobacco taxes is estimated to have cost Canada more than $14 billion in tax revenue. U.S. border states have also recently increased tobacco taxes, thereby giving Canada room to increase its taxes to earlier levels.

Another negative impact of the tax cut is that it contradicts directly the widely recognized finding that increases in prices discourage youth from smoking. The federal government has also failed to undertake a national anti-smoking education campaign aimed at preventing youth from smoking. At the same time, tobacco companies have been circumventing Canada's ban on tobacco advertising by sponsoring arts and sporting events, many of them aimed at youth.

BANNING LANDMINES
NOBEL PEACE PRIZE FOR CITIZEN CAMPAIGN AND FIRST COUNTRY TO RATIFY INTERNATIONAL TREATY

It is estimated that 24,000 people, most of them civilians, are killed or maimed by landmines every year worldwide. Large amounts of land in some countries cannot be used for agriculture and development because of minefields. In addition, declining populations of animals such as Asian elephants in Sri Lanka, apes in central Africa, silverback gorillas in Rwanda, and snow leopards in Afghanistan are further threatened by deaths caused by landmines.

In December 1997, after years of educational work and lobbying by over 1,000 non-governmental groups from 75 countries, an international treaty banning the use, stockpiling, export, and manufacture of anti-personnel mines was signed in Ottawa by 122 countries, including 33 countries that formerly produced the mines. The treaty became international law after Canada, and then 39 other countries that had signed the treaty, ratified it. As of March 1, 1999, 66 countries in total had ratified the agreement.

As a result of the treaty, armies in Africa, Europe, and North America have started to destroy their stockpiles of landmines. The biggest producers of landmines, China, Russia, and the U.S., have not signed the treaty yet, but since the treaty was signed they have all enacted export bans. The treaty also states that countries that are in a position to help, such as Canada, must help other countries clear mined land and provide for the care of landmine victims.

In Canada, the campaign to eliminate anti-personnel landmines is led by Mines Action Canada, a member of the 1998 Nobel Peace Prize-winning International Campaign to Ban Landmines.

F O O D

DEVELOPMENT OF CANOLA PLANT VARIETIES FOR EDIBLE OIL

Rape and turnip rape, relations of turnips, rutabagas, and cabbage, are vegetables that produce an oil from their seeds that has come to be known in Canada as canola oil. Rapeseed oil was used as a lubricant in steam engines in the 1800s, and later for boat engines. However, it was not grown commercially in Canada until the Second World War, when supplies from Europe were cut off.

After the war, Dr. Burton Craig, a researcher at the National Research Council's laboratory at the University of Saskatchewan, Dr. R. Keith Downey, a scientist with Agriculture Canada in Alberta and Saskatchewan, and Baldur Stefansson, a plant breeder and professor at the University of Manitoba, began working together to produce a Canadian variety of rapeseed oil. Although the oil from plants related to rapeseed had been used as a cooking and burning oil in China and India for over four thousand years, clinical studies had revealed potential problems because the oil contains erucic acid, associated with heart lesions in animals, and glucosinolates which cause enlarged thyroids and other problems in livestock. As a result, the oil was normally not used for cooking in Europe or North America. Craig, Downey, and Stefansson, along with many others, first identified low-erucic acid and low-glucosinolate varieties of the rape plant, and then successfully reproduced these strains over a twenty-year period from 1957 to 1977.

By 1967, 2.6 million hectares of land in Canada were devoted to production of the first viable strains of canola, and the development of even better strains. By 1977, the low-glucosinolate varieties were developed and canola for livestock meal began to be produced in large quantities. Canada is now the third-largest exporter of canola, producing 25 per cent of the world supply and over $1 billion in annual revenues since 1981. Canola oil is widely used in Canada and Europe as a cooking oil, and in margarine, salad dressing, and shortening. After the oil is extracted, the remaining material is used as a high-protein feed for livestock.

In 1976, Downey was appointed an Officer of the Order of Canada, as was Stefansson in 1985.

WALTER CHELL
INVENTOR OF THE BLOODY CAESAR DRINK

It may not be considered a food by many people, but it has been described as Canada's national cocktail. An immigrant from Montenegro in the 1950s, Walter Chell was working for the Westin Hotel chain in Calgary in 1969 when he spent three months perfecting the Bloody Caesar cocktail. The drink was first made with clams Chell mashed himself and mixed with tomato juice, and of course vodka, Worcestershire sauce, salt, and pepper.

The Mott company later developed canned "clamato" juice that mixed clams and tomato juice, and after a dispute with Chell about the drink he invented, Mott hired him to consult and promote the company's products.

Chell began working in the hotel business in Switzerland, and he left Canada in the early 1970s to work in South Africa. He later returned to Canada, where he worked at the Hotel Toronto, retiring in 1990. He died in 1997.

HOWARD DILL
DEVELOPED WORLD'S BIGGEST PUMPKIN SEED STRAIN

From the time he was a small child, Howard Dill, along with his sisters Maxine and Margaret, helped his parents work their vegetable and dairy farm in Windsor, Nova Scotia, as had many generations in his family before him. His father's 170-kilogram-plus giant pumpkins were an attraction at the local agricultural exhibition, one of the oldest in North America, but little Howard could not have known then just how giant his pumpkins would become.

Born July 22, 1934, in Windsor, Dill was a member of the local 4-H Club as a young boy, and although he raised calves for local show competitions, he began to focus more and more on pumpkin growing as he grew older. Although he had no formal training in plant breeding, he tracked characteristics of several pumpkins, noting seeds that produced larger pumpkins, and over time he began to produce remarkable results.

By 1969, Dill was growing pumpkins weighing over 440 kilograms. These were not record-setting pumpkins, however, as Charles Hewitt, also from Nova Scotia, had set the world record in 1883 with a 505-kilogram pumpkin. Through cross-breeding, hand-pollinating, and ongoing experimentation, Dill eventually developed an open-pollination variety he called Dill's Atlantic Giant.

He obtained protection of his seed strain, and proceeded to win four consecutive world championships for giant pumpkin growing from 1980 to 1984, with the largest weighing in at 1,088 kilograms in 1981. Since then, cash prizes of up to $50,000 have been offered each year at pumpkin growing competitions, and Dill's seeds have been used to grow winners of more than 2,200 kilograms since 1996.

Dill sells more than 2,000 pounds of seeds each year through distributors around the world, and fills another 5,000 individual orders from his farm.

WORLD'S BIGGEST BOWL OF STRAWBERRIES

In 1995, Marylou McGill organized an event in Kitchener, Ontario, that, somewhat surprisingly, had also been held in Ireland, England, Sydney in British Columbia, and Portage la Prairie in Manitoba since 1989.

In each case, participants in the event were attempting to put as many strawberries as possible into one bowl. With much needed help from Joe Moss of Moss Berries Ltd., McGill's event set a world record by stuffing 2,372.29 kilograms of strawberries into a huge bowl, beating the previous record of 2,174 kilograms by an unhealthy margin.

WORLD'S LARGEST LENTIL EXPORTER

The lentil, which comes in many varieties, is a vegetable (or legume) that has been recognized as a good source of protein. Prior to 1964, lentils were not produced in Canada, but that year the federal government provided subsidies to farmers to switch to alternative crops to reduce wheat production. Canada has expanded production since 1964 to become the second-largest lentil producer in the world, after India. In 1983, production was 55,000 tonnes; by 1998 it had increased to 479,000 tonnes.

Lentils are probably not found on many dinner plates that often across the country, given that Canada exported 374,086 tonnes of our production in 1998, thereby surpassing Turkey as the largest lentil exporter in the world. Saskatchewan, Manitoba, and Alberta are the main lentil-growing provinces in Canada, and their level of production is expected to continue to increase in the future.

ENVIRONMENT

C ANADA'S ENVIRONMENT
FOREMOSTS IN THE WORLD

Canada's environment sets records all by itself, some impressive, some amazing in the respect that someone stuck around to measure them. According to the *Guinness Book of World Records*, the strongest water currents, moving at 29.6 kilometres per hour, are found in the Nakwakto Rapids in the Slingsby Channel in B.C. In addition, the highest tides in the world are found in the Bay of Fundy, in Nova Scotia. The world's largest bay is Canada's Hudson Bay, based upon the length of its shoreline, while the world's largest lake, Lake Superior, lies half in Canada and half in the United States.

The coldest temperature ever recorded in North America was -63 degrees Celsius at Snag, in the Yukon Territory, on February 3, 1947. The same temperature was reached at Mayo, also in the Yukon Territory, but it was not officially recorded so Snag holds the record. The record is not exactly an attribute to boast about in order to attract tourists, and Snag has proven this in that at the time it was essentially an airport strip, not an actual community, and now it is abandoned.

Another record came with more than a little help from the environment. In February 1988, during Winnipeg's Festival du Voyageur, a group of Canadians set the record for the world's largest snowman, building a creature 15.6 metres tall. They held the record very briefly however, as a group of Americans in Anchorage, Alaska, built a 19.3-metre snowman one month later. The new record, with a 27.4-metre snowman, is now held by residents of Saas-Fee, Switzerland.

FIRSTS IN ANIMAL POPULATION STUDIES

The comprehensive knowledge of aboriginal peoples around the world about animal habits, and environmental issues in general, has been well documented in many cases, and in some cases is just beginning to be documented. Ecologists have learned many things from aboriginal peoples, and have also explored other aspects of the environment using classic scientific techniques. Canadian ecologists and others working in Canada have recorded world firsts in understanding animal populations, as detailed below.

WILLIAM RICKER – DEVELOPED RICKER CURVE TO TRACK FISH POPULATIONS

His hometown was Waterdown, Ontario, and it couldn't have been more aptly named given his future career. Born August 11, 1908, William Ricker studied the stars and looked for birds in the woods as a young boy near his home. His early studying set the basis for Ricker to obtain undergraduate, master's and doctoral degrees in biology by 1936, all from the University of Toronto.

During his summers, Ricker worked for the Ontario Fisheries Research Laboratory. After graduation, he became a professor of zoology at Indiana State University, but soon returned to Canada to become Chief Scientist of the federal Fisheries Research Board. In 1938, he participated in the first survey by the Canadian Salmon Commission of sockeye salmon in the Fraser River, B.C., and since then he has kept track of the surveys' results.

In the 1950s, Ricker developed the Ricker Curve, a means of determining what average maximum catches should be set for fisheries in different regions in order to sustain fish populations at healthy levels. The Curve incorporates several possible causes, which Ricker first proposed, for the variation in returning salmon stocks that occurred in cycles. For example, the Fraser River sockeye population rises and falls on a four-year cycle, and Ricker first speculated that the changes may occur because most of the fish mature at four years of age. The Ricker Curve is still used all over the world.

Ricker is now retired, although he still monitors developments at the Nanaimo Biological Station of the Canadian Department of Fisheries and Oceans. Among many other awards he has received, in 1970 Ricker was made a fellow of the Royal Society of Canada, in 1986 he was appointed to the Order of Canada, and in 1990 he was named an Eminent Ecologist by the Ecological Society of America.

DENNIS CHITTY – WORLD'S EXPERT ON LEMMINGS

One of the first scientists to undertake animal ecology studies in the world, Dennis Chitty is the author of many papers on the regulation of numbers of natural populations of animals. Born September 18, 1912, in Bristol, England, Chitty came to Canada in 1930 for his undergraduate studies, obtaining his degree from the University of Toronto in 1935.

Chitty obtained his master's from Oxford University in 1947, and his doctorate in philosophy in 1949, and then returned to Canada to teach at the University of British Columbia. For over sixty years, Chitty has studied animal populations, and his studies are cited in all textbooks on ecology. He is regarded as the world's expert on lemmings.

Chitty won, among many other awards, a Master Teacher Award in 1973, and the 1988 Fry Medal from the Canadian Society of Zoologists, and he is now Professor Emeritus of Zoology at the University of British Columbia.

WORLD'S FOREMOST ULTRAVIOLET LIGHT WATER-DISINFECTION EQUIPMENT

In 1977, Hank Vander Laan heard about a disinfecting system for water treatment that used ultraviolet (UV) light. Invented by a man named Harry Lewis, the system shines UV light on bacteria, viruses, moulds, algae, and other micro-organisms in water, altering these organisms so they cannot reproduce, and as a result they die off and the risk of disease from them is eliminated. Vander Laan researched the system, and heard encouraging words from regulators and experts in the field about the potential for such a system to replace chlorination as a disinfectant.

At the time, studies of chlorination had discovered that chlorine reacts with organic material in water, and while it disinfects effectively, it also creates by-products that cause cancer in humans at a fairly high rate.

Along with partner Kelly Jarmain, Vander Laan bought the company, called Trojan Technologies, from Lewis, even though none of Lewis's systems had ever sold. Most cities in North America remained committed to chlorination of drinking water, despite the health hazards, mainly because of the cost of replacing their disinfectant systems.

Before becoming involved in the water disinfectant industry, Vander Laan had spent fifteen years helping build the cable TV business of Rogers Communications, and he put his engineering and sales experience to work with his new company. As awareness grew of the negative effects of chlorination (also including the dangers of handling chlorine, and high operating costs for chlorination systems), and of the effectiveness of UV light as a disinfectant, Trojan's operations expanded to meet growing demand.

Based in London, Ontario, and with offices in the Netherlands, England, and the U.S., Trojan has become the world leader in sales of UV light disinfection systems. They have over 2,000 systems in municipalities in over twenty-five countries, over 3,000 systems in use by various industries, and over 100,000 households using their residential systems.

WILLIAM (BILL) LISHMAN
FIRST PERSON TO FLY WITH AND LEAD A MIGRATION
OF A FLOCK OF BIRDS

Migration is a learned behaviour for birds, and so birds that are threatened or endangered can easily lose their ability to migrate if they are scattered across the country without any older birds to lead them. This situation can further threaten the birds if unusual weather or other environmental conditions affect their home, especially in the winter, and they have no ability to fly south to a more favourable climate.

Scientists have been worried about just such events threatening the existence of the few remaining whooping cranes in the world. There are only about 400 whooping cranes left, and only 183 migrate together in a flock.

In the mid 1980s, after an accidental flight in an ultralight plane with a flock of ducks, William Lishman began taking steps that eventually may help save the whooping crane and other endangered birds. From 1985 to 1988, Lishman experimented with help from his two sons and daughter, eventually succeeding in leading a flock of twelve geese with an ultralight in July 1988.

Through a process called imprinting, Lishman was able to make goslings believe that he was their primary caregiver by hatching them in an incubator and acting as a surrogate parent for several months. His first flight with the flock led to further experiments over the next five years.

In October 1993, Lishman and his assistant, Joseph Duff, with help from Dr. William Sladen of Virginia, successfully led a flock of 18 geese in an ultralight over a 644-kilometre journey from Ontario to Virginia. The next spring, 13 of the 18 geese returned on their own to Ontario. In October 1994, Lishman and Duff led another 38 geese south 1,287 kilometres to South Carolina, and of these 34 returned to Ontario in April 1995. The experiment was repeated in the fall of 1995 with 30 geese from Ontario transported by truck across the border and then led to Virginia, where another 29 geese had been raised. Of the 30 geese led south, 14 returned to Ontario in spring 1996.

In 1995, Lishman began working with sandhill cranes, successfully raising three cranes and leading them on short flights around Ontario. Late that year Lishman's autobiography, *Father Goose*, was published and it became a best-seller. In the fall of 1996, the feature film *Fly Away Home*, based on Lishman's work, was released. Lishman worked as a consultant and stunt double on the film, roles to which he brought a wealth of experience as he had made an award-winning video of his first flights with geese in 1988.

In the fall of 1997, the team led seven cranes to Virginia, six of which returned the next spring. The team found that the cranes were too familiar with humans, however, and so over the summer of 1997 they focused on raising fifteen cranes differently, trying to keep them as wild as possible. Instead of leading the cranes in a full migration, in October 1998 the team transported them by truck south to Virginia, and then led them with ultralights the final 160 kilometres to South Carolina. Four of the cranes were lost due to various mishaps through the trip and the winter, and the team did not expect the others to return since they had not been shown the full migration path.

When Lishman first suggested and began experimenting with leading birds in flight, scientists were very sceptical. Now, through their non-profit group Operation Migration, Lishman, Duff, and Slaken are connecting with scientists around the world. A nesting site has been set up in Wisconsin in the hopes of establishing a new flock of migrating whooping cranes, and Operation Migration will be involved in the future in attempts to imprint, train, and lead the flock in a migration. In addition, there are plans underway to lead a flock of endangered Red Crowned cranes in a migration in Japan.

DR. INGE RUSSELL
INVENTOR OF SUPER YEAST FOR FUEL ALCOHOL

Scientific research often yields unintended results, and the story of super yeast is a compelling example. In 1980, Inge Russell was entering her second decade at the research department of the Labatt

Brewing Company Ltd. in London, Ontario. She first joined the company in 1970 after studying as a medical technologist, and intended to move to a hospital to do genetic research. However, her initial work at Labatt's on genetic variations of yeast caught her interest, and she stayed.

Russell and her colleagues were trying in the early 1980s to produce an improved yeast strain for beer production that could, among other things, ferment faster, would create a better flavour, and could utilize starch to produce a lighter beer. The production process involves selecting yeast strains of opposite types, a and alpha (essentially male and female), and mating them through a process called micromanipulation; letting the cells that result grow into spores, then mating them with other genes that, for example, give the yeast the ability to ferment starches. Russell then used a new technique that had just been discovered by other scientists called "spheroplast fusion" that allows strains that would never mate in nature to be fused together.

Throughout the process, the cells created are tested to ensure they have the desired genetic qualities. Another hurdle is to create cells that are stable, so that they will not change characteristics through the process of brewing beer or in other industrial processes.

One of the yeast strains that Russell was able to isolate turned out to be totally stable, contained the desired genes, and fermented faster than any strain she had ever seen before, in other words, a "super yeast." The only problem was that one of its qualities meant that beer produced using it would taste like a disinfectant, not exactly a desirable quality. However, its fast fermentation and ability to tolerate high temperatures made the super yeast perfectly suitable for fuel alcohol production.

Since Labatt's is not in the fuel alcohol business, after patenting the yeast strain around the world between 1984 and 1989 they sold the strain to the Lallemand Yeast Company. Lallemand is one of the largest yeast producers in the world and they now successfully sell Russell's strain to the fuel alcohol industry around the world. Fuel alcohol is a renewable resource which burns cleaner than gasoline, and its use is growing as a substitute for fossil fuels in developing countries in particular.

Labatt's has funded Dr. Russell's ongoing education throughout the past twenty-eight years, allowing her to study part-time for a Bachelor of Science between 1972 to 1981, and in Scotland for a Master's of Science from 1981 to 1983, a Ph.D. from 1982 to 1988, and a D.Sc. in 1997. Russell has registered another first as well, as she was elected as the first woman president of the American Society of Brewing Chemists in 1990. Since 1997, she has been the Manager of Technology Planning & Innovation at Labatt's.

LOTEK ENGINEERING INC.
DEVELOPED NEW TECHNOLOGY FOR TRACKING WILDLIFE

Before 1984, the tracking of wildlife was difficult, especially for animals that range over large areas, travelling faster than human observers can and in areas where machines cannot easily be used to monitor the animals' behaviour. Historically, the collection of data involved repeated capture and release of animals or even killing the animals to obtain physical data.

However, three people came together in 1984 to form Lotek Engineering, based in Newmarket, Ontario, and have developed the first automatic tracking system that solves all the historical problems. Using Global Positioning System (GPS) receivers, which bounce signals off satellites, radio controls, and communications links, and a data storage unit, Lotek's system provides high accuracy positioning of animals at all times.

Lotek was started with financing from the people involved and other individuals, along with support from the federal National Research Council and Industrial Research Assistance Program (IRAP). Its innovations began in 1988 when the company created, at their St. John's operation (Lotek Marine Technologies Inc.), the first implantable fish electromyogram transmitter capable of recording and transmitting metabolic activity and energy expenditure data. In 1989, the first receiver for land-based animals was developed. As it has grown through the 1990s, Lotek has developed software to support their hardware, including laser-configurable data collection and validation strategies, adaptive frequency scanning, summary record generation and real-time statistical analysis, diagnostic and fault-recovery strategies, and remote-system monitoring with upload/download control via phone lines.

In 1994, Lotek received the excellence award from the Canadian Awards for Business, given by the National Quality Institute and Industry Canada, in the small business category. Since then, it has gone on to achieve other innovations. In 1995, it developed the automatic large mammal tracking system using GPS receivers, and in 1999 it produced the world's smallest digitally encoded fish transmitter, along with the first fish tag fully integrated into a receiver system.

Lotek now employs about sixty people in total at its two locations. Lotek has also entered a partnership with National Sciences and Engineering Research Council of Canada (NSERC) to sponsor a faculty position at the University of Waterloo to further the theoretical research side of wildlife management and conservation. Fifteen graduate students work with the professor.

FIRSTS IN REDUCTION OF CHLORO-FLUOROCARBONS (CFCs)

The effects of chlorofluorocarbons (CFCs) are considered to be one of the world's most important environmental issues. CFCs deplete the ozone layer of the Earth's atmosphere, which shields us from the sun's ultraviolet rays. Ultraviolet rays have been established as causing skin cancer and cataracts in humans, as well as suppressing human immune systems and damaging crops. One CFC molecule can destroy 100,000 ozone layer molecules.

Before 1992, about 10 per cent of the CFCs released into the atmosphere were from the manufacturing process of the electronics industry. CFCs are also used and released by many other industries and products. In January 1992, officials at the Canadian telecommunications company Northern Telecom announced that they had eliminated a step in their electronics manufacturing process that used CFCs. The company thereby became the first major electronics company in the world to stop using CFCs.

As of 1988, about one thousand tonnes of CFCs were used by Northern Telecom in its forty-two plants around the world to clean excess flux from circuit boards. Flux helps seal solder joints that held electronic parts to the circuit boards. By reducing the amount of flux used to a fine mist, and then boiling it off later in the manufacturing process, Northern Telecom no longer needed CFCs to clean the circuit boards. According to Northern Telecom, the new process cost $1 million to develop but has saved the company an estimated $50 million. Since 1992, the company has shared its expertise with companies around the world.

In recognition of its reduction of CFC use, Northern Telecom received awards from the U.S. Environmental Protection Agency in 1991 and 1997. The company also received the United Nations Environment Program's Best-of-the-Best Stratospheric Ozone Protection Award on September 16, 1997, ten years after the "Montreal Protocol" international agreement to eliminate CFC emissions was reached. The Montreal Protocol, signed by over 160 nations to date, sets the year 2000 as the target for the phase-out of CFC use worldwide.

Another Canadian first in the area of CFC emissions was the development of "Blue Bottle" technology. Co-inventor Dusanka Filipovic, an engineer, was working as an executive at the Linde Division of Union Carbide (now Praxair Canada Inc.) in Canada when the technology was developed from 1986 to 1991.

The key to the Blue Bottle technology is a synthetic zeolite (trademarked as Halozite) which selectively adsorbs halogenated hydrocarbons such as CFCs. The system eliminates virtually all emissions of refrigerant in a wide variety of processes, including routine purging of refrigeration and air conditioning equipment during service and decommissioning.

Adsorption is a phenomenon where molecules of the CFCs stick on a solid surface. In the Blue Bottle cylinder, the modified zeolite acts as a filter, capturing only refrigerant while other chemicals are left untouched. The technology captures CFCs at room temperature, which eliminates the need for special vehicles and licensing to use the equipment.

When the technology was developed, Union Carbide did not manufacture or market CFC products, nor was it involved in recycling. The company decided to license the technology in order to ensure it was developed and marketed quickly, and as co-inventor at the company, Filipovic was chosen as licensee. She started up and is Deputy Chair of Halozone Technologies Inc. Halozone has raised $13.5 million through the stock market, and is also supported by $900,000 in grants over three years from the Ontario Government's Ministry of Environment and Energy, and a $2.5-million grant from Canada's Environmental Technologies Commercialization Program.

Once a Blue Bottle cylinder has been filled with CFCs, it is sent to Halozone's central facility outside of Toronto which has been operating since 1994. There, the CFCs are reclaimed and returned to industry standards before being transferred to storage containers. The Halozite adsorbent and the cylinders can be reused. Halozone makes the technology in several different sizes for use by individuals and companies, and it can also be used to capture other toxic substances, such as methyl bromide, which is used as a fumigant in agriculture, and halon, which is used as a fire retardant.

Halozone also markets a technology that improves the efficiency of refrigeration equipment, thereby reducing energy use and operating costs.

SCIENCE

GEORGE KLEIN
MULTIPLE MECHANICAL ENGINEERING INVENTIONS

George Klein has been called one of Canada's most prolific inventors for good reason. Born in 1904 in Hamilton, Ontario, Klein grew up exploring a watch factory housed in the same building as his father's jewellery business. He studied mechanical engineering at the University of Toronto, graduating in 1929. He was then invited by a former professor to join the National Research Council's research facility, which had just been set up in Ottawa.

For the next four decades until he retired, Klein worked on many innovative projects. He played a major role designing the NRC's wind tunnel. He also researched the properties of snow and designed efficient plastic-coated aircraft skis for bush aircraft. During the Second World War Klein invented and developed many items to aid the Allied war effort, including improved sights for guns and safety mechanisms for detonation devices, and he served on the multi-nation committee that designed the Weasel, an all-terrain vehicle.

Near the end of the war, Klein steered a team in designing the Zero Energy Experimental Pile (ZEEP), the first atomic reactor outside the U.S., located at Chalk River, Ontario. Given the recent tragic and unfortunate history of nuclear reactors in Canada and the world, Klein may not have viewed his design work on this project as a notable part of his legacy.

His most well-known invention is the Storable Tubular Extendible Member (STEM), a retractable antenna Klein developed in the early 1950s to guide aircraft to bombing targets. The STEM was used on the Alouette, Canada's first satellite, and on every Gemini spacecraft launched by the U.S. National Aeronautics and Space Administration (NASA) program. The STEM is still standard equipment on satellites.

Also in the early 1950s, Klein invented the electric wheelchair for use by quadriplegics, and wheelchairs available today are based on his original design. His team also developed a surgical instrument for mechanically stitching severed arteries.

In the 1960s, Klein began examining how to make gears for aircraft and ships more efficient. This early work eventually led to Spar Aerospace asking Klein to help design the gearing system for the Canadarm in 1976. Canadarm is a fifteen-metre-long mechanical arm used by pilots on the U.S. space shuttle to move cargo and make adjustments on the outside of the shuttle. (See the history of the Canadarm in *Canada Firsts*, and an update in the Introduction of this book).

From 1959 and on after his retirement, Klein lectured at Carleton University in the mechanical engineering department. He was appointed to the Order of Canada in 1968, and also received an honorary doctorate from Wilfrid Laurier University that year. In 1988, he received an honorary doctorate from Carleton University.

Klein died in Ottawa on November 4, 1992, at age eighty-eight, acknowledged by many as the greatest mechanical design engineer Canada has ever produced.

DAVIDSON BLACK
LEADER OF DISCOVERY OF PEKING MAN

In his boyhood, Davidson Black enjoyed searching for fossils around his neighbourhood in Toronto, where he was born in 1884. His fascination with fossils continued into his adult life, and led to the discovery of a critical link in the evolution of the human species.

Black studied medicine and arts at the University of Toronto. His focus on anatomy and the brain led to a teaching position in neurology in Cleveland. He also served in the Canadian Army Medical Corps during the First World War.

After the war, Black obtained a posting as a professor of anatomy at the Peking Medical Union College in Peking (now Beijing), China. While in Asia he took the opportunity to concentrate his own studies on prehistoric humans, as this region of the world was rich in fossils. Indeed, many ancient humanlike teeth were reportedly found in Chinese medicine shops, although they were considered to be dragon's teeth with special properties that helped cure specific diseases. The teeth came from excavations of fossils but they had not been systematically analyzed.

At a scientific meeting in 1926, two Swedish scientists reported the discovery of two of the "dragon's teeth," and in response the Crown Prince of Sweden proposed an expedition to the site of the discovery near the village of Zhoukoudain (forty kilometres southwest of Peking). Black was appointed leader of the expedition, which was funded by the Rockefeller Foundation.

The expedition team excavated a site called "Dragon Bone Hill" but after months of work by many people only one tooth was found. As digging continued in 1927, however, a number of caves were unearthed and the team uncovered a skull. Back at his laboratory, Black made plaster-cast copies of the skull, and named the fossil "Peking Man" in honour of its country of origin.

From other fossil evidence, it was determined that Peking Man was *homo erectus,* the first of our species to walk upright. Further discoveries revealed that the inhabitants of the caves likely also used tools made of quartz and were the first to use fire.

In 1934, Davidson died at the laboratory he helped found in China, and was found collapsed over one of the fossils collected from many excavations. At the time, the laboratory's collection of 175 specimens representing forty prehistoric individuals was the largest collection ever of early human fossils.

A few years after the Second World War started, an effort was made to move the laboratory's collection to the U.S. Marine Guard for protection. The collection was boxed up and loaded on the ocean liner *President Harrison* but the fossils never left port as the ship was captured by the Japanese. The original collection of fossils has not been seen since, but fortunately the plaster casts Black made survived intact. As a result, many copies of the Peking Man fossils are found in museums around the world, evidence for millions of people to see of the origins of humans.

DONALD COXETER
WORLD'S GREATEST LIVING GEOMETER

Harold Scott MacDonald (Donald) Coxeter was born in London, England, on February 2, 1907. He was educated at boarding school, and in his teenage years won a prize for an essay on a geometric problem. This early sign of Coxeter's talent with geometry caught the eye of an English mathematician, who arranged for Coxeter to leave boarding school and receive two years of coaching in mathematics. Coxeter's original interest was in music and composing, but this two-year training launched him firmly into a career exploring triangles, cubes, rectangles, and many more complex shapes.

In 1926, Coxeter began his studies at Trinity College, Cambridge, and emerged from there several years later with a doctorate in mathematics. He spent two years as a research fellow at Princeton University, and in 1936 received an invitation to become an assistant professor at the University of Toronto. He decided, after consulting with his father and G. H. Hardy (a famous British mathematician and mentor) to take the offer. Escaping the coming war and turmoil in England, Coxeter and his bride, Hendrina, headed for Toronto, where they still reside.

Over the past sixty years, Coxeter has written twelve books and has had 167 articles published. He is best known for contributions to the Theory of Polytopes (shapes that exist in two, three, four, or more dimensions and can't be drawn but can be described mathematically), Non-Euclidean Geometry, Discrete Groups, and

Combinatorial Theory, as the areas of mathematical research are known. In 1926 he discovered a new regular polyhedron (a geometrical shape) having six hexagonal faces at each vertex. In 1933, Coxeter set out in number form n-dimensional kaleidoscopes (the variations on possible shapes and forms that could be viewed through a multi-dimensional kaleidoscope).

He is best known for, and most proud of, his discovery of something called "inversive distance." When two intersecting circles drawn on a plane overlap, or even if they do not overlap, Coxeter discovered that the angle at which they meet is always dependent on the distance from the centre to the side of each circle (each circle's radius), and the distance between the centres of the circles.

The mathematics or, more accurately, the geometry, Coxeter practises may not have immediate applications to the everyday world, except perhaps in art. For example, in early 1999 Coxeter examined *Circle Limits III,* one of his friend M. C. Escher's drawings, and found that it was mathematically perfect, even though Escher knew little about mathematics and had done the drawing by hand and with simple instruments. Other mathematical theories exist for years before any application is found for them. For example, Group theory was originally just an exercise for mathematicians, but it eventually was found to be the perfect means for describing subatomic particles.

Coxeter is a Fellow of both the Royal Society of London and the Royal Society of Canada, and a Companion of the Order of Canada, the highest honour awarded in Canada for lifetime achievement.

FIRSTS AND FOREMOSTS IN RESEARCH INTO FUNCTION OF THE BRAIN

Canadians and people working in Canada have achieved several firsts and foremosts in research on the human brain. Donald Hebb has been an influential person in these discoveries, and in modern neuroscience overall.

DONALD HEBB – DISCOVERER OF THE HEBB SYNAPSE

Born in Chester, Nova Scotia, Hebb wanted to be a novelist, and decided to study psychology to help his writing. His studies led him in another direction, first to a master's in psychology from McGill University of Montreal, then a Ph.D. from Harvard in 1936, and culminated in the publication of *The Organization of Behaviour* in 1949. Hebb's book proposed that neural structures in the brain, which he called cell assemblies, are formed by feedback through what is now called the Hebb synapse. The theory guided his landmark experiments on the influence of early environment on adult intelligence, and also laid a basis for neural network theory, an area of research in artificial intelligence.

RONALD MELZACK – DISCOVERER OF THEORIES AND TESTS OF PAIN

Dr. Hebb, who had discovered the Hebb synapse, eventually became Chair and Chancellor of psychology at McGill University, where he continued his work until his death in 1985. Back in 1954, Hebb was mentoring Ronald Melzack, a doctoral student who had been born in Montreal on July 19, 1929. After he obtained his Ph.D. from McGill, Melzack worked with people who experience pain in limbs that have been amputated, so-called "phantom-limb" pain. He began collecting and classifying words patients used to describe pain. In 1965, Melzack was at the Massachusetts Institute of Technology (MIT) when, along with colleague Patrick Wall, he developed the gate-control theory of pain. According to their theory, how people experience pain is influenced, or filtered, by past experience. The theory led to the discovery of endorphins and enkephalins, painkillers created by the body.

In 1975, and back at McGill, Melzack took all the pain words he had collected and created the McGill Pain Questionnaire, which is now used in pain clinics and cancer hospices around the world to test patients' response to pain, and to determine effective treatments.

An author of several books and articles and winner of many prizes,

Melzack is now Research Director at the Pain Clinic of the Montreal General Hospital, and the E. P. Taylor Chair and professor in Pain Studies in the psychology department at McGill. His recent research indicates that there are two types of pain, transmitted by two different pathways in the central nervous system. Sudden, short-term pain, such as the pain from a cut, is transmitted by a group of pathways that Melzack calls the "lateral" system, because they pass through the brain stem on one side of its central core. Long-term or chronic pain is transmitted by the "medial" system, whose neurons pass through the central core of the brain stem.

DOREEN KIMURA – WORLD EXPERT ON SEX DIFFERENCES IN THE BRAIN

Another foremost Canadian in research on the brain is Doreen Kimura, who was inspired by an introductory course taught by Donald Hebb at McGill. Born in 1940 in Winnipeg, Manitoba, Kimura grew up in Saskatchewan and, after dropping out of high school at age seventeen, was working as a teacher in a one-room rural schoolhouse when she decided to apply to McGill for an admission scholarship in response to an advertisement in a teaching magazine.

Kimura went on to obtain her Ph.D. in psychology at McGill in 1962. She spent two years in postdoctoral work at the Montreal Neurological Institute, and then studied at the University of California at Los Angeles (UCLA) Medical Center and the Zurich Kantonsspital in Switzerland. In 1967, she became a professor of psychology at the University of Western Ontario.

Kimura's area of study, of which she is the world expert, is the influence of sex and hand preference on specific functions of the brain. She has developed many neuropsychological tests for determining impacts, and has a small consulting business for selling the tests. For example, as Kimura's tests have shown, on average men can match rotated objects faster than women, but women are better at matching objects based on their surroundings. Also, speech disorders occur most often in women when they have brain damage in the front of the brain, while in men they occur when the damage is in the back of the brain.

A recipient of many honours and awards, Dr. Kimura is also a Fellow of the Canadian Psychological Association, the American Psychological Association, the American Psychological Society, and the Royal Society of Canada.

HANS CHRISTIAN FIBIGER – DISCOVERED CAUSE AND TREATMENT FOR DEPRESSION

Born in Denmark, Hans Christian Fibiger moved to Canada and obtained his undergraduate degree in science from the University of Victoria in B.C. in 1966, and then his Ph.D. at Princeton University in 1970. In 1972, he became a professor of psychiatry at the University of British Columbia, and began researching depression.

Dr. Fibiger and colleagues in his laboratory discovered that neurons in the midbrain contain the neurotransmitter dopamine, and that dopamine is an essential part of the electrochemical process in the brain by which humans experience pleasure. As a result of Fibiger's research, treatment of depression has come to include drugs that attempt to balance dopamine levels in the midbrain.

Fibiger was awarded the 1993 B.C. Science and Engineering Gold Medal Award in Health Sciences. He is among the two hundred most frequently quoted scientists in any field in the world.

BERTRAM N. BROCKHOUSE
NOBEL PRIZE WINNER FOR INVENTION OF ATOMIC PARTICLE ANALYZER AND STUDIES

For researchers studying microscopic atomic particles in the middle of the century, an ongoing problem was that the wavelength of ordinary light is wider than many of the particles being studied, and so the light either obscured or distorted the particles. For example, a hydrogen nucleus is one angstrom in width, whereas light is 7,000 angstroms wide.

Canadian Bertram N. Brockhouse solved this problem in the early 1950s. Brockhouse, born July 15, 1918, in Lethbridge, Alberta, grew up there and in Vancouver. When he was seventeen, his family moved to Chicago, hoping to find a better situation than in Depression-era B.C. He had learned how to design, build, and repair radios and started a business when his family returned to Vancouver in 1938. Brockhouse enlisted in the Royal Canadian Navy in 1939 and spent most of the Second World War servicing radio equipment. With his postwar government funding, he entered the University of British Columbia and graduated with a degree in physics and mathematics in 1948.

After working at the National Research Council in Ottawa during the following summer, Brockhouse entered the University of Toronto, graduating with a Ph.D. in physics in 1950. From there he went to work at the Chalk River Nuclear Facility north of Ottawa. At that time, experiments were being developed to determine the physical attributes of many materials by sending beams of neutrons into the materials. Brockhouse and his colleagues focused on experiments involving the physics of solids such as metals and crystals, an area called solid-state physics.

To overcome the many barriers to observing how neutrons were scattered when they collide with the materials on an atomic level, Brockhouse invented the Triple-Axis neutron spectrometer. He constructed the spectrometer using a neutron beam with a wavelength of one to four angstroms, which allowed for much more detailed study of atomic particles. The spectrometer also allowed the direction and intensity of the neutron beam, the position of the specimen, and the angle and sensitivity of the detector to be adjusted. This flexibility greatly increased the number of possible ways of studying particles with the same machine.

In 1962, Brockhouse took a position as a professor of physics at McMaster University, in Hamilton, continuing his experiments there along with teaching courses. For his invention, which is now used worldwide to study the structure of crystals, his experiments, and the development of methods for analyzing results of neutron-scattering experiments, Brockhouse shared the 1994 Nobel Prize in Physics with American Clifford G. Shull. He has also been named a Fellow of the Royal Society of Canada, an Officer of the Order of Canada, a foreign member of the Royal Swedish Academy, and a Fellow of the Royal Society of London. He was also named Professor Emeritus at McMaster University, and is now retired and living with his family in Ancaster, Ontario.

RAYMOND U. LEMIEUX
FIRST TO SYNTHESIZE SUGAR AND MANY OTHER SUBSTANCES

Raymond Lemieux was born in Lac La Biche, Alberta, on June 16, 1920. His parents were poor and he had a difficult life growing up in Edmonton. However, Lemieux's sister had a friend who was a graduate student and inspired Lemieux to attend university. He obtained his undergraduate degree in chemistry from the University of Alberta, and then his Ph.D. in organic chemistry from McGill University.

Lemieux then undertook postdoctoral studies at Ohio State University, studying the degradation of the antibiotic streptomycin. His work in this area led him to be the first person in the world to synthesize sucrose, or sugar. In 1955, he invented a chemical reagent with another scientist, the first of many reagents he would go on to invent (reagents are substances used in chemical reactions to test for the presence of other substances). In 1973, Lemieux began to work on the synthesis of human blood, and eventually he synthesized the carbohydrate sequences for seven different blood group determinants. His discoveries made it much easier to produce synthetic blood products for use in scientific research.

Among many other awards, Lemieux won the 1991 National Sciences and Engineering Research Council of Canada (NSERC) Gold Medal for Science and Engineering, NSERC's highest honour, and the 1992 Albert Einstein World Award in Science. He is now Professor Emeritus of Chemistry at the University of Alberta.

SIDNEY ALTMAN
NOBEL PRIZE FOR DISCOVERY OF CATALYTIC PROPERTIES OF RNA

Sidney Altman was born in Montreal on May 8, 1939. His boyhood heroes included, among others, ice hockey stars and Einstein. He attributes his early interest in science to the explosion of the A-bomb and the questions surrounding scientists involved in its development.

Altman planned to enter McGill University after high school, but ended up at the Massachusetts Institute of Technology studying physics. Just before beginning his graduate studies at Columbia University, Altman was exposed to the new field of molecular biology, and two years later he switched out of physics and began examining characteristics of deoxyribonucleic acid (DNA) under the direction of others at the University of Colorado Medical Center.

DNA is a molecular material that nearly all living organisms contain, and it carries information about the genetic tendencies of each organism. Another Canadian, Oswald Theodore Avery, played a key role in discovering DNA. Born in 1877 in Halifax, Nova Scotia, Avery was educated at Columbia University's College of Physicians and Surgeons. In the early 1940s, Avery and his colleagues conducted an experiment that involved extracting a substance from a bacterium with a smooth surface and introducing it into a rough-surfaced bacterium. The result was that the rough-surfaced bacteria changed into the smooth-surfaced type. At the time, biochemists believed that the substance responsible for these kind of genetic changes was a protein. However, the substance extracted in Avery's experiment was DNA. The findings of the experiment were first published in 1944, and it led to more intensive studies of DNA, which eventually confirmed that DNA was the key genetic agent. Sidney Altman's research work, along with the work of many other scientists, was a direct extension of the pioneering work of Avery, who died in 1955.

After his time at the University of Colorado, Altman moved to Harvard to continue his studies of types of DNA, and two years later he considered himself lucky, as an ex-physicist, to join an elite team of researchers at the Medical Research Council Laboratory of

Molecular Biology in Cambridge, England. While there he started research work on the characteristics of ribonucleic acid (RNA), a molecule that builds proteins in cells, essentially following the genetic instructions contained in DNA.

His research work led to a job at Yale University in 1971, and through the 1970s Altman studied how the genetic code of DNA was transcribed into RNA. It was thought at the time that the process required enzymes and other proteins to act as biocatalysts for the transcription, and that all enzymes were proteins (made up of amino acids). What he and American Thomas Cech discovered, independently of each other, was that DNA itself acts as a biocatalyst for the transcription process.

They made this discovery, Altman in 1978 and Cech in 1982, by examining two different, specific enzymes that were transcribing DNA instructions on RNA. The enzymes were made up of protein and RNA molecules, and when the molecules were separated, the enzymes were no longer functional. Both discovered that the RNA molecules could function on their own as catalysts. Many different types of catalytic RNA, or ribozymes as they have come to be called, have been discovered, and it is hoped that they can be used to destroy RNA molecules that produce harmful or undesirable properties in organisms, such as viruses.

For their discovery of the catalytic properties of RNA, which came as a complete surprise to the scientific world, Altman and Cech were awarded jointly the 1989 Nobel Prize in Chemistry.

RICHARD E. TAYLOR
NOBEL PRIZE FOR DISCOVERY IN PARTICLE PHYSICS

As detailed in *Canada Firsts*, Ernest Rutherford won the 1908 Nobel Prize in Chemistry for his work at McGill University in Montreal, and became the leader in atomic physics when he set out his famous model of the atom in 1911.

Since then, knowledge of the atomic nucleus has greatly increased. In the 1930s neutrons were discovered, and then it was discovered that the atomic nucleus consists of protons and neutrons, making them, along with electrons, the building blocks of nature. Then the characteristics of protons and neutrons (known as nucleons) were explored in depth (see "Bertram N. Brockhouse" above), and in the process new particles were discovered in the 1950s, called hadrons, which resembled neutrons. This threw the fundamental nature of nucleons into doubt, although hadrons were a mystery as well. The structure of hadrons was explained in the early 1960s to the satisfaction of many physicists when the theory of three building blocks for the particles, called quarks, was developed. However, experiments attempting to confirm the existence of quarks were unsuccessful.

A research team led by Jerome I. Friedman and Henry W. Kendall, both of the Massachusetts Institute of Technology, and Canadian Richard E. Taylor of Stanford University, undertook to prove the existence of quarks in the late 1960s and early 1970s.

Taylor, born November 2, 1929, in Medicine Hat, Alberta, travelled a long way physically and intellectually to become part of this leading team. He was not an outstanding student in high school, and although he specialized in mathematics and physics at the University of Alberta, he struggled to keep up with other students when he entered the graduate physics program at Stanford University. His experimental work was impressive, however, and in 1958 he was invited to join a group of physicists in Paris who were constructing an electron accelerator for experiments in Orsay, France. In 1961, Taylor returned to the U.S., and participated in the construction of the two-mile-long Stanford Linear Accelerator Center (SLAC), also for electron-scattering experiments.

Electron accelerators provided a new way of looking at atoms. Previously, beams of electrons moving at relatively slow speeds were aimed at protons and neutrons, and it was thought that sufficient knowledge about protons and neutrons had been gained from observing the effects of these collisions.

However, when the SLAC-MIT experiments were conducted, it was found that electrons moving at high velocities collided with an inner structure in protons and neutrons. The evidence of the inner structure was believed to confirm the existence of quarks as the building blocks of protons and neutrons and, therefore, of all matter on Earth. According to the results of these experiments, more than 99 per cent of all matter is quarks along with gluons, the glue that holds the quarks together, while the remaining 1 per cent is electrons.

For leading the research team to these discoveries, which introduced a new era in the history of physics, Friedman, Kendall, and Taylor shared the 1990 Nobel Prize in Physics.

RUDOLPH A. MARCUS
NOBEL PRIZE FOR ELECTRON TRANSFER THEORY

Rudolph Marcus, born in 1923 in Montreal, was enamoured with school from a young age. He attended Baron Byng High School in the city, and then went on to McGill University for both undergraduate and graduate degrees in chemistry, receiving a Ph.D. in 1946. From there, Marcus joined the then-new postdoctoral program at the National Research Council in Ottawa. It was the beginning of theoretical work in chemistry and many other scientific areas in Canada.

In 1948, Marcus applied and was accepted for postdoctoral work at the University of North Carolina in Chapel Hill. Under the direction of Oscar K. Rice, a well-known theoretician, Marcus undertook many experiments and published several leading papers on chemical theories. In 1951, he secured a faculty position at the Polytechnic Institute of Brooklyn.

From 1956 to 1965, Professor Marcus developed his theory based on one of the simplest chemical elementary processes, the transfer of an electron between two molecules. An increase in energy is needed in the molecules and their nearest neighbours to enable the electrons to jump between the molecules. The size of the energy barrier determines the speed of the chemical reaction. Marcus's theory, a simple mathematical formula, allowed calculations and explanations to be developed of the energy barriers of many chemical reactions involving electron transfers.

His theory was controversial at the time because in some cases it predicted things that conflicted with the expectations of many chemists, and the predictions were difficult to confirm in experiments. Amazingly, some of his theoretical predictions could not be confirmed until the late 1980s.

Marcus also taught at the University of Illinois at Urbana-Champaign from 1964 to 1975, and then at the California Institute of Technology from 1978 on. For his contributions to the theory of electron transfer reactions in chemical systems, Marcus was awarded the 1992 Nobel Prize in Chemistry. He has received numerous other awards and honorary degrees and is a member of the National Academy of Sciences (since 1970), the American Academy of Arts and Sciences (since 1973), an honorary member of the Royal Society of Chemistry (since 1991), and a member of the Royal Society of Canada (since 1993).

DEVELOPMENT OF MICRO-DETECTION EQUIPMENT

As detailed in *Canada Firsts,* in the 1980s Canadian Dr. Lorne Elias of the National Research Council invented the Explosives Vapour Detector (EVD), which uses gas chromatography analysis equipment to detect the presence of minute amounts of explosives. Other detectors, using different types of analysis technology, have also been invented by Canadians.

MDS SCIEX – DEVELOPED MASS SPECTROMETER DETECTORS

In the 1960s, Barry French, an engineering physics professor, Neil Reid, a chemist who had worked at NASA, and Adele Buckley, a graduate student, were working together at the Institute for Aerospace Studies at the University of Toronto. They were helping with development of a mass spectrometer to be carried by the Viking space probe to analyze gases in the upper atmosphere of Mars. At the time, French began to think about other uses for the technology.

Mass spectrometers analyze samples of gases, liquids, and solids, revealing the makeup of the sample on a microscopic level. French saw possible uses for spectrometers on Earth, such as tracking pollutants, detecting explosives, and diagnosing diseases that show up in the breath, if the equipment could be developed.

They found that it was possible to develop a prototype that could do something completely new by taking a sample of air, placing it in a vacuum, ionizing the molecules in the sample, and identifying microscopic substances in the air within a few minutes. In the early 1970s, the three of them mortgaged their homes and, with two business partners, invested $100,000 to start a company called Sciex to manufacture and sell this technology. They applied for, and received, an important $200,000 development grant from the federal government.

As they began to spread the word of their technology, Sciex sold units to laboratories and industries around the world. They always faced challenges with cash flow, however, as profits were devoted to further research and development. In 1981, MDS Inc., a Canadian company, took a key step when it bought Sciex, providing much-needed capital for further developments. As MDS Sciex, the company entered into a joint venture in 1986 with U.S. Perkin-Elmer Corp., a large manufacturer and distributor of analytical equipment that helped greatly with marketing and sales. And again government funds helped out, as an Ontario technology fund matched $17 million in capital raised by Sciex to improve its products between 1987 and 1992.

MDS Sciex now makes many different instruments that can identify substances in various forms as small as 1/1,000,000,000,000,000,000 of a gram in size. Their technology is used mainly in laboratories. The company is now headquartered in Concord, Ontario, and employs 375 people. Its products are marketed by Perkin-Elmer under the brand name PE Sciex, and most recent annual sales are more than $225 million to twenty-five countries. In April 1999, MDS Sciex, in partnership with the National Sciences and Engineering Research Council of Canada (NSERC) and York University announced the creation of a $2.37 million research position in analytical mass spectrometry at York. MDS Sciex will contribute $720,000 in equipment and $500,000 over five years to the position.

BARRINGER TECHNOLOGIES – DEVELOPED ION MASS SPECTROMETER DETECTORS

Anthony Barringer and his colleagues are among the key people in the development of another micro-detection technology. Born in England on October 20, 1925, Barringer was trained in geophysics and geochemistry at Imperial College and worked as a geologist in the British military. He was sent to Canada in the 1950s to prospect for mineral deposits by the Selection Trust Mining Group, a large British mining conglomerate.

He became a Canadian citizen, and through the next three decades he invented many techniques for ore and oil exploration through his company Barringer Technologies (see "Firsts and foremosts in mineral exploration" below in *Business* chapter). In the early 1970s, his colleague John Davies used his contacts to diversify the company into explosives detection. Davies, also from Britain, was trained as a physicist. He came to Canada in 1965 and worked with Westinghouse Canada for two years on military equipment development. He wanted to do something beneficial for civilians and started working with Barringer.

With funding initially from the British government, and then from the Royal Canadian Mounted Police, the company began to explore explosives detection techniques. In the early 1980s, with further funding through development contracts from Canada Customs and Transport Canada and from U.S. government agencies, Barringer eventually adapted ion mobility spectrometer (IMS) technology for this new use, as well as for drug detection.

Originally developed in Britain for use by British military in chemical weapon detection, IMS differs from the EVD's gas chromatography and Sciex's mass spectrometry in that it involves the collection and analysis of ions, or particles of the substance to be detected, rather than the analysis of larger samples of gases, liquids, or solids for all their component parts. The process developed by Barringer involves heating the collected particles to high temperatures (turning them into vapour) and then analyzing them in portable ion detectors.

In 1990, after almost two decades struggling to convince sceptics that ion particles of substances could be collected and analyzed, Barringer produced its first eight detectors. Since then, the company has demonstrated that its equipment can detect plastic explosives, which are undetectable by the EVD or mass spectrometry.

INTELLIGENT DETECTION SYSTEMS (IDS) – COMBINED DETECTION TECHNOLOGIES

In the early 1980s, Colin Corrigan retired from the federal government where he had worked for several years in a division overseeing shipyard building. A former merchant marine, Corrigan then went to work with his brother at Corrigan Instrumentations, an X-ray equipment company in Toronto. In 1985, the Air India bombing tragedy occurred, and it created a demand for X-ray equipment to scan passengers and luggage at airports for bombs.

Corrigan decided to look at other bomb detection methods, and in 1986 set up CPAD Holdings Ltd. with others to explore the area. With funding from individuals and venture capitalists, CPAD contracted with researchers at Carleton University in Ottawa to develop the technology. Further funding came through a grant from an Industrial Research Assistance Program (IRAP), with oversight and support provided by Dr. Lorne Elias at the National Research Council (NRC) and by the RCMP.

CPAD has developed a combined gas chromatograph (GC) and IMS system. The company initially developed walk-through detectors for screening passengers, but other airplane bombings in the late 1980s involving bombs in luggage and other cargo focused development on a system that could scan large volumes of cargo. Further funding to develop such a system came in 1991 from Transport

Canada, its Transport Development Centre, and the U.S. Federal Aviation Administration (FAA).

In April 1995, Dr. Mariusz Rybak and his son Andy Rybak took over the company and the name changed to CPAD Technologies. The following year it merged with an integrated engineering company, and in November 1997 the new company came to be called IDS Intelligent Detection Systems. IDS, based in Nepean, Ontario, issued shares in the stock market a short time later and raised over $30 million.

Since then, IDS has expanded into several different detection industry areas, and has eight offices around the world. In the summer of 1998, the company took over Scintrex Ltd., the company that made the EVD under licence from the National Research Council (NRC), as detailed in *Canada Firsts*. As a result, IDS now markets the latest version of the EVD, the EVD-3000, which is a handheld narcotics detector. Other Scintrex products now marketed by IDS are the NDS-2000, a handheld explosives detector, and Scintrex's mining exploration products and services (see piece on Harold Seigel in "Firsts and foremosts in mineral exploration" in the *Business* chapter).

Currently, IDS has developed the third generation of its Orion and Orion Plus GC/IMS detectors, and they are in use in several countries. In early 1999, the company sold the first six units of its new invention, the Large Vehicle Bomb Detection System (LVBDS), which is used as a screen for car bombs.

DEVELOPMENT OF LIQUID MERCURY TELESCOPE (LMT)

In the late 1700s, and maybe earlier, scientists discovered that the surface of a spinning liquid is the shape of a paraboloid, in other words, curved in the same way as the mirrors used in telescopes. However, early attempts to build liquid mirrors for use in telescopes, dating back to the mid 1800s, were abandoned because of the difficulties of creating a surface that would reflect images accurately.

The fact that such a mirror could not be tilted also discouraged scientists' efforts.

In 1983, Ermano Borra, a physics professor at the University of Laval in Quebec, published a paper investigating the liquid mirror concept. Borra and his colleagues at Laval, Dr. Robert Content and Ph.D. student Luc Girard, concluded after early tests that building liquid mirrors was possible, and worthwhile.

Mercury is used for liquid mirrors because it reflects images very clearly. The mercury is contained in a shallow paraboloid made of lightweight composite material for large mirrors or simple plywood discs for mirrors with a diameter of one metre or less. The paraboloid is supported on a stand that is stabilized using a three-point mount that aligns the axis of rotation parallel with the gravitational field of the earth. The smaller mirrors are supported on air bearings, but oil-lubricated bearings are used for larger mirrors as they can support a greater mass due to their rigidity. The mirror spins on a belt-and-pulley system driven by a motor. This system allows the operators to control the speed of the spinning disk and thereby control the focal point of the mirror.

In colloboration with Paul Hickson of the University of British Columbia, Borra and his colleagues built one of the first practical liquid mercury telescopes, with a diameter of 1.5 metres. Since then, they have constructed mirrors with diameters of 2.5 metres and 5 metres for use by their own universities, the U.S. National Aeronautics and Space Administration (NASA), the University of Western Ontario, and the University of California at Los Angeles (UCLA).

Although the mirrors cannot be tilted, they are used in astronomy and atmospheric science for tracking specific parts of the sky as the earth rotates. Liquid mirrors are less expensive to build than conventional mirrors, and have very high surface quality and a variable focus that can be controlled with high precision. As a result of the high quality of the surface of the mirror, they are also used for optical testing.

BIRUTE GALDIKAS
WORLD'S FOREMOST AUTHORITY ON ORANGUTANS

Birute Galdikas was born in Germany on May 10, 1946, as her parents were on their way from Lithuania to Canada. Her migratory early days may have predisposed her to explore the world and the history of humans, but Galdikas credits her childhood days exploring High Park, in Toronto, where she grew up, following and observing animals for hours at a time, with setting her on the path to her life's work.

In her undergraduate studies in psychology and biology, through to her doctorate in anthropology, which she obtained from UCLA in 1978, Galdikas pursued her interest in the evolution of humans. In 1968, Galdikas met the famous Dr. Louis Leakey, who discovered fossils of early humans in Africa. With his help, and the assistance of the National Geographic Society, Galdikas set up a research camp in Borneo to study orangutans.

Since the mid 1970s, Galdikas has split her time between living in the jungle observing orangutans and teaching at Simon Fraser University in B.C. She has learned more about orangutans than any other person, most importantly that they like to be left alone. Adult male orangutans roam up to forty square kilometres of jungle, sometimes for weeks without seeing any kin.

As an anthropologist, Galdikas has applied her studies to understanding human nature, concluding that the life of the orangutan, while stable, is solitary and anti-social. Humans evolved and progressed, Galdikas believes, because we socialized with others in families and communities, developing tools, language, and social institutions. According to her, it is in society's interest to promote families and communities because, in accordance with our biological heritage, these social structures discourage natural animal greed and encourage mental well-being in humans.

Galdikas has founded orangutan support groups all over the world. In 1993, Galdikas won a United Nation's Global 500 Award for her research on orangutans.

DISCOVERY OF THE ALBERTOSAURUS AT WORLD'S FOREMOST DINOSAUR FOSSIL SITE

In 1884, twenty-five-year-old geologist Joseph Burr Tyrrell was working for the Canadian Geological Survey in southern Alberta, exploring and mapping the land south of Drumheller, a 116,500-square-kilometre area. Far from his birthplace in Weston, Ontario, Tyrrell had obtained the job after his doctor advised him to find outdoor work. He was paddling down the Red Deer River with his assistant on June 9 when they discovered a fossilized skeleton of a dinosaur.

It turns out that Tyrrell had uncovered the first remains of what came to be called the Albertosaurus. A close relation to the fierce Tyrannosaurus Rex, an adult Albertosaurus could be up to nine metres long and weigh as much as two tonnes. Scientists estimate that the dinosaur became extinct about seventy million years ago.

Since then, the area of Tyrrell's discovery has proven to be the world's most important dinosaur fossil site for examining the social behaviour of the Tyrannosaurus Rex family. Now known as Dinosaur Provincial Park, it has been designated a world heritage site by the United Nations. Fossils of more than 475 dinosaurs have been found in the region, although until recently only eight were Albertosaurus skeletons, and the staff of the Royal Tyrrell Museum of Paleontology in Drumheller continue to search for more.

In August 1997, Dr. Philip Currie, head of research at the museum, and his colleagues made a discovery that only added to the site's notoriety. They were following the few clues left behind by Barnum Brown, a prominent paleontologist and discoverer of the first Tyrannosaurus Rex skeleton in Montana in 1902. Brown had travelled by barge down the Red Deer River every summer from 1910 to 1916, collecting railway cars full of fossils along the way. His field notes indicated that during his first trip he had discovered a specific site full of fossils, but had not returned to explore the site further.

In 1996, Currie travelled to Brown's old workplace, the American Museum of Natural History in New York, to examine his collection. He found fossils of the right feet of nine Albertosauruses, and this discovery and a few of Brown's photos led him and his team to spend ten days retracing Brown's barge trip down the river. On the second day of their trip, the team came across traces of one of Brown's old campsites. Intense heat had worn out half the team, and so Currie explored the surrounding area on his own.

As he explored several canyons and ridges, Currie was about to give up and was running out of water when he found the spot from which Brown had taken one of his photographs. He returned to the team's campsite with the news, and the next day he returned with the others and found signs of over thirty full Albertosaurus skeletons. Since their discovery, the excavation on the site has begun, although some remains will be left for future scientists to examine, in their original state, with what will likely be more advanced techniques than are available today.

SAFETY

IMPROVED FINGERPRINTING TECHNIQUES

As detailed in *Canada Firsts*, Dr. Lorne Elias of the National Research Council developed the Explosives Vapour Detector, which greatly improved safety at airports around the world. In 1990, Elias and his colleagues at the NRC developed another technique for improving safety, a better method of detecting and photographing fingerprints.

Often, fingerprints at crime scenes are difficult or impossible to obtain. First, researchers at the NRC developed an improved vacuum chamber for creating the low-pressure environment that allows for more efficient gassing of fingerprints with vaporized cyanoacrylate (the substance used in high strength glues). Once the fingerprints are coated with cyanoacrylate in the vacuum chamber they are treated with a fluorescent dye and exposed to a portable fluorescent light, also developed by NRC. The resulting prints are a brilliant yellow, making them much easier to photograph.

ADVANCES IN CARDIOPULMONARY RESUSCITATION (CPR) TREATMENT

CARLA HANSON – INVENTOR OF CPR POSITION AID

Canadians have developed two major advances in cardiopulmonary resuscitation (CPR) treatment. First, Carla Hanson applied her experience as an attendant on air and land ambulances to invent an aid for locating the proper position for applying CPR. Hanson grew up in Baudette, Minnesota, and later moved to Dryden, Ontario. Much of the land in northern Ontario around Dryden is wilderness crisscrossed by rough roads, and journeys by ambulance are often slow.

In 1984, Hanson had great difficulty administering CPR to a farmer who had collapsed in his field during the half-hour trip to the hospital in Dryden. She looked into various methods for solving the problems she had, and in 1988 was issued a Canadian patent for the Landmarc (named after the "landmark" or proper position on a person's chest for applying CPR).

The Landmarc is a plastic mat that quickly and easily adheres to the patient's skin, accurately marking the proper position and providing a good grip which makes the application of CPR more effective. Its effectiveness has been proven by the fact that, without extensive marketing, 25,000 Landmarcs are sold worldwide annually by MTM Health Products.

Hansen found support for developing her invention from a service program at Lakehead University in Thunder Bay, Ontario, which helped her with industrial design and to select a Winnipeg plastics manufacturer. The Innovation Centre in Waterloo, Ontario also helped with an assessment of the device.

DEVELOPMENT OF FOREMOST CPR TRAINING MANNEQUIN

Another aid for CPR was developed by three graduates of the Carleton University School of Industrial Design, Richard Brault, Dianne Croteau, and Jonathan Vinden. They recognized the need for an economical, effective CPR training mannequin, and teamed up with a patent lawyer to form a new company, Actar Airforce Inc., to develop the product. By the early 1990s, the result of their efforts, the ACTAR 911 CPR Training Mannequin, was being praised and used worldwide.

ACTAR 911 was developed after examining the needs of CPR instructors. It has only six parts, all easy to clean and recyclable, in contrast to the more than one hundred of many past training mannequins. Also, a carrying case that would have held one traditional mannequin can be packed with ten ACTAR 911 mannequins, and yet weigh only half as much.

Within one year of being on the market, the ACTAR 911 became the number-one-selling CPR mannequin in Canada and the U.S. The device has also been exported to many countries around the world. In 1991, Actar Airforce was awarded the Canada Award for Business Excellence in the category of industrial design and in 1992 the company won a Financial Post Design Effectiveness award.

WENDY MURPHY
INVENTOR OF STRETCHER FOR TRANSPORTING INFANTS

In 1985, Wendy Murphy was home watching the news after a shift at the Hospital for Sick Children (Sick Kids) in Toronto where she worked as an X-ray technician. She saw coverage of the Mexican earthquake and took special notice of an image of a tiny infant being transported on an adult-sized stretcher, with little protection from falling off. She grabbed a pencil and made a sketch of a baby-scale stretcher, but put it aside. Two years later, a fire at Sick Kids that almost forced the evacuation of several babies from the neonatal intensive care unit, where Murphy was then working, prompted her to take another look at her sketch. At a staff meeting the next day, Murphy presented her idea to the immediate approval of hospital administrators.

At the insistence of Dr. Barry Smith, head of pediatrics at the hospital, Murphy spent the next two years designing and developing the Weevac, a stretcher with pockets and straps for holding up to six infants. Since then, she has developed a version for outdoor rescues, among other rescue equipment, all with help from the Innovation Centre in Waterloo, Ontario.

The Weevac is currently widely used in Canada, the U.S., New Zealand, Japan, and England. For her invention, Murphy won the 1992 Manning Award and the National Research Council 75th Anniversary Award for innovation in medical device technology.

FOREMOST COMPUTER DATABASES OF VIOLENT CRIMES AND BULLET TYPES

Following several cross-Canada investigations of serial homicides in the mid 1980s, most notably the Clifford Olson case, Canadian law enforcement officials decided to set up a nationwide database to collect data on violent crimes. They were not the first, as the U.S. Federal Bureau of Investigation (FBI) already had an automated linkage system for such cases. However, the Canadian version has come to be recognized as the foremost in the world.

The first attempt to link cases in Canada was called the Major Crimes File (MCF), but it did not work very well, and so in 1991 development of what would come to be called the Violent Crime Linkage Analysis System (VICLAS) began. Several U.S. systems were reviewed, including the FBI database, and experts in behavioural science were consulted to create a list of 262 questions that investigators attempt to answer about each case they are tracking. All solved or unsolved homicides and sexual assaults, missing person cases, unidentified bodies that are believed to be homicide victims, and non-parental abductions are included in the Canadian system.

Sergeant Keith Davidson of the Violent Crime Analysis Unit in British Columbia had developed an early version of a database for the province. Based on his experience, he was recruited as a consultant along with Inspector Ron MacKay (head of the Violent Crime Analysis

Branch at RCMP headquarters and Canada's first trained and qualified Criminal Investigative Analyst), Sergeant Greg Johnson, Sergeant Sharon Oliver in Ontario, Sergeant Gerald Seguin in Quebec, and computer experts John Ripley and Paul Leury. Over 20,000 cases are in the VICLAS database, which has been running since February 1996, and it is maintained by sixty specially trained officers.

According to Dr. David Cavanaugh of Harvard University, who was a consultant to the FBI in developing its system, Canada's database is the best in the world. Australia, Austria, Belgium, Holland, the United Kingdom, and U.S. states Tennessee and Indiana have all adopted the Canadian system, and other countries are in the process of setting up databases based on VICLAS.

Despite its excellence, the system has been hampered by the lack of participation of investigators, who have seemingly failed to learn any lessons from cases such as the series of rapes committed in Scarborough and the murders committed in the Niagara region by Paul Bernardo. Even after Bernardo was finally arrested, the two police forces involved did not cooperate with each other in their investigations. In response to a court review of that investigation, Ontario passed a law requiring all police officers to file cases with VICLAS, but other provinces have yet to follow suit. Another problem with the system is chronic understaffing, which has hindered efforts to keep the system up-to-date.

In a related development, Forensic Technologies of Montreal created a computer program in the early 1990s that can compare standard ballistic "fingerprints" of thousands of types and calibres of bullets with bullets collected at crime scenes. The program can compare more than one thousand bullets an hour, which would have taken ballistic experts thousands of hours in the past. The software, called IBIS, and selling at $500,000, has been bought by many U.S. city police forces, as well as by forces in Asia, Eastern Europe, Egypt, Israel, Russia, and South Africa. Canadian police forces do not use the program because of the small number of firearms-related crimes in the country.

DAVE McCUE
INVENTOR OF FIRE HOSE BRACE

Twelve years of volunteer firefighting provided Dave McCue with plenty of stories of struggling with high-pressure fire hoses. One particularly cold night, ice collected at the end of the hose and McCue and his colleague struggled to hold on. It occurred to McCue that a brace of some sort would have helped enormously.

He began with a drawing, then worked through $50,000 of his savings and several prototypes, from a ten-kilogram steel design to a two-kilogram heavy-duty plastic brace that attaches to the end of the hose. Another $200,000, and help from Sommerville Design and Manufacturing of Pickering, Ontario, lowered the weight of the device to one-and-a-half kilograms.

Beyond his significant financial investment, McCue spent five years applying for a patent and trying to attract the interest of firefighting forces at hundreds of trade shows, all on his own time. As he refined the brace, McCue added a handle that helps firefighters carry hoses at the scene of a fire. He calls the device the EZ PUP (for "easy performance under pressure").

In 1997 McCue was nominated for a Manning Award, and although he didn't win, the ensuing publicity, along with tests by the U.S. Navy and orders from fire departments in several European countries and Sweden, finally helped McCue cover some of his debts. Mobil Corporation purchased thirty EZ PUPs, and through 1998 over 2,500 EZ PUPs were sold in thirty-two countries.

A R T S

C ASAVANT FRÈRES LTD.
WORLD'S FOREMOST ORGAN MANUFACTURER

Trained as a blacksmith, Joseph Casavant left his business at the age of twenty-seven (in 1834) and undertook a classical education at a seminary in St. Hyacinthe, Quebec. While there, Casavant was asked to repair the seminary's organ by the director. His successful work caught the attention of a local church, and he received his first commission to build an organ in 1840.

By 1866, Casavant had produced sixteen other organs. One organ he built for the Catholic cathedral in what was then Bytown (now Ottawa) was the largest in North America at the time. The organ consisted of 1,063 wooden and metal pipes, eighty-five octave stops, and a three-keyboard console. Unfortunately none of these organs are around today.

Casavant died in 1874. His two sons, Claver and Samuel, who had been formally trained in Europe in organ-making, together started up Casavant Frères Ltd. in St. Hyacinthe in 1879 to continue building organs.

Since then, the company has been at the forefront of organ manufacturing and development. Throughout the early part of the 1900s, with the help of Englishman Stephen Scott, the company developed many technical improvements that set the industry standard and are the hallmark of Casavant organs. In 1930, the brothers were awarded the Grand Prix at the International Exhibition held that year in Antwerp, Belgium. The company has also adapted to electronic devices that are often found in modern-day organs.

At the same time, the company restores and maintains its organs around the world, many of which are over one hundred years old and still in use. For example, the massive eighty-two-stop organ with adjustable combinations and nine-metre-tall speaking pipes at the Notre-Dame Church in Montreal, the first organ the brothers built, continues to produce high-quality music. Casavant organs have been installed in the U.S., Mexico, South America, throughout Europe, the West Indies, South Africa, Australia, and Japan.

The company has built more than 3,700 organs, and 90 per cent of them are exported. The 1996 installation of a monumental Casavant Opus 3750 organ with 129 stops and 10,615 pipes at Broadway Baptist Church in Fort Worth, Texas, is typical of the prestigious commissions the company continues to receive.

FIRSTS AND FOREMOSTS FOR FILM PRODUCERS, DIRECTORS, ACTORS, AND TECHNICIANS

Several Canadians have become movie stars and won Academy Awards for their performances including, for best supporting actor, Harold Russell in 1946 for his performance in *The Best Years of Our Lives*, Walter Huston for his role in *The Treasure of the Sierra Madre* in 1948, and Graham Greene for his role in the 1990 film *Dances With Wolves*. Anna Paquin of Winnipeg won an Oscar for her 1993 role in *The Piano*, and Canadian-born director James Cameron won several awards for his 1997 film *Titanic*, the highest grossing film ever.

In film, as with many of the arts, determining who is foremost is a very difficult task. A few Canadians and people with connections to Canada, however, have risen to foremost-in-the-world status through a lifetime of achievements, including a few firsts along the way. Their stories are set out below.

LOUIS B. MAYER AND JACK WARNER –
MOST POWERFUL HOLLYWOOD PRODUCERS

Although they lost touch with the country at a relatively young age, the lives of legendary movie executives and producers Louis Burt Mayer and Jack Warner have Canadian connections.

Born Eliezer (Lazar) Mayer on July 4, 1885, in Minsk (now in the former Soviet republic of Belarus), Mayer's family moved to Saint John, New Brunswick, when he was three. Before he was a teenager, Mayer began working at his father's scrap-metal business. At age nineteen, Mayer moved to Boston, Massachusetts, and set up a similar business.

In 1907, he bought and renovated a run-down cinema in Haverhill, Massachusetts, and began showing only top-quality films. His one-theatre operation soon grew to be the largest chain in New England, and in 1914 he added film distribution to his business. After making a large profit from distributing legendary director D. W. Griffith's controversial film *The Birth of a Nation,* Mayer moved to Los Angeles and formed his own production company.

By 1924, after a series of mergers, Metro-Goldwyn-Mayer (MGM) was formed and Mayer became chief of production. Until 1951 he would rule as the most powerful producer in Hollywood, discovering many of film's greatest stars, directors, and writers while earning the highest salary of anyone in the U.S. He played a key role in founding the Academy of Motion Picture Arts and Sciences in 1927, and was also active in politics, serving as the state chairman of the California Republican Party for several years. Mayer was forced out of his position at MGM in 1951, and died in 1957.

One of the people Mayer hired in 1934 was Sydney Guilaroff, who also had Canadian connections and would become known as "the man with the golden shears." Guilaroff was born in England and grew up in Winnipeg and Montreal, but he left at age fourteen for New York. He found a job sweeping floors in a hair salon, but learned the trade quickly and was soon cutting and styling at Antoine's, one of the top salons in the city.

When actress Joan Crawford made him her personal stylist he

gained national attention and left for Hollywood. He would serve as MGM's top stylist until 1971, and among other notable activities he dyed Lucille Ball's hair red, styled Elizabeth Taylor's hair for the film *National Velvet,* was flown to Monaco for Grace Kelly's wedding day, and proposed to Greta Garbo after a lengthy affair. He was rejected by Garbo, and never spoke to her again, nor married. In 1938, Guilaroff became the first single man to adopt a son, and in later years he adopted a second son and a former employee. He died of pneumonia on May 28, 1997.

Jack Warner was born August 2, 1892 in London, Ontario, the youngest of twelve children. His parents were Jewish immigrants from Poland who moved around the U.S. and Canada before settling in Youngstown, Ohio. After opening a cobbler's shop, a butchery, and then a bicycle shop, the Warner family bought a nickelodeon in Newcastle, Pennsylvania, in 1903. Two years later, Jack and four older brothers began distributing films, but they were taken over by another company.

The first short films they tried producing in 1912 were also not very successful, but in 1917 they finally had a hit with the film *My Four Years in Germany.* A few years later they established Warner Bros., which soon became one of Hollywood's major studios. Jack became production chief, and his first major achievement was launching the sound era in 1927 with the film *The Jazz Singer.*

Warner would go on to work, and quarrel, with actors Bette Davis, Olivia De Havilland, Humphrey Bogart, and James Cagney, among many others. He was well-known as a practical joker, but also as stubborn and difficult at times. Two of his brothers, Harry and Albert, sold most of their shares in the company in 1956. Jack remained as studio boss and largest single stockholder. In 1959, he was given the Irving G. Thalberg Memorial Award at the Academy Awards in recognition of his lifetime achievements as a producer. In 1967, Warner sold his shares in the family company and became an independent producer.

DOUGLAS SHEARER – FOREMOST FILM SOUND TECHNICIAN

Douglas Shearer, a native of Montreal, played a key role for Jack Warner on the first sound film, *The Jazz Singer*. A film technician focusing on sound recording, Shearer went on to win the first Academy Award in the Sound category in 1930 for the film *The Big House*. That year his sister, Norma Shearer, won the Best Actress award for the film *The Divorcee*.

Shearer was nominated almost every year for an Academy Award in the Sound category for the next two decades, and he won four more times. He also won other technical Academy Awards, and his twelve Oscars in total are the most won by any Canadian.

MARY PICKFORD – MOST POPULAR, AND WEALTHIEST, ACTRESS

Norma Shearer's 1930 Academy Award win was preceded by Toronto-born Mary Pickford's, who won for best actress in 1929 for her role in the film *Coquette*, and followed by Ontario-born Marie Dressler's win in 1931 for the film *Min and Bill*. Born Gladys Louise Smith on April 8, 1892, Pickford was a successful child actor on Broadway. In 1908, she signed a studio contract, moved to Hollywood, and became the undisputed queen of the screen for twenty-three years. According to surveys at the time, Pickford was the most popular woman in the world for fourteen of those years, and was known as America's Sweetheart (and in Europe as the World's Sweetheart).

She married leading man Douglas Fairbanks and in 1919 helped start United Artists Studios with him, D. W. Griffith, and Charlie Chaplin. It was a radical move, as actors were controlled by the major studios at the time, but typical of Pickford, who made several creative and lucrative business deals in her career and became the first woman to earn one million dollars a year in the industry.

Pickford also helped found the Motion Picture and Television Fund charity. In 1936, Pickford divorced Fairbanks, and a year later married musician and actor Buddy Rogers, with whom she would spend the rest of her life. Her home in Hollywood, called Pickfair for her and Fairbanks, was the hub of social activity for decades.

Pickford appeared, often in a starring role, in 245 films between 1908 and 1942, and produced or helped write another thirty-five films. She always credited her mother, Charlotte, for providing key support and guidance that helped her become so successful. In 1976, in her last public appearance, Pickford accepted a Lifetime Achievement Award at the Academy Awards ceremony. She died on May 29, 1979. In May 1999, a star on Canada's Walk of Fame in downtown Toronto was dedicated to Pickford.

NORMAN JEWISON – FOREMOST PRODUCER AND DIRECTOR

Born July 21, 1926, in Toronto, Ontario, Norman Jewison studied music and theatre during his high school days. He served in the Royal Canadian Navy during the Second World War, and afterwards returned to school, obtaining his undergraduate degree at the University of Toronto in 1950.

Jewison drove a taxi while trying to build a career as a stage and radio actor, and even moved to London, England, briefly to write scripts and act for the British Broadcasting Corporation. He returned to Toronto and soon was a leading director of TV programs for the Canadian Broadcasting Corporation (CBC). In 1958, he left for New York for three years to direct musical variety shows for many stars, including Frank Sinatra, Harry Belafonte, Danny Kaye (on Kaye's television debut), and for *The Andy Williams Show*, and Emmy award-winning Judy Garland specials.

In the early 1960s, Jewison turned his formidable producing and directing skills to feature films. He was soon recognized as a major talent and a powerful commentator on American society. His 1966 film *The Russians Are Coming! The Russians Are Coming!* was released at the height of the Cold War and provided a satirical look at the global situation, humanizing both sides of the conflict. In 1967 as the civil rights movement was in full force in the U.S., he released *In the Heat of the Night*, which dealt with race relations and included the first showing in film of a black character slapping a white character. The film won five Academy Awards. These films and Jewison's 1971 film *Fiddler on the Roof,* 1984's *A Soldier's Story,* and 1987's *Moonstruck,* were all nominated for best director or best picture, although none won. Jewison's films have won ten Oscars out of the forty-eight nominations they have received.

In 1986, Jewison established the Canadian Centre for Advanced Film Studies, which has since trained and supported many of the country's filmmakers. His high level of achievement in film was recognized on March 21, 1999, when he was awarded the Irving G. Thalberg Memorial Award at the Academy Awards. It was the thirty-first time the award had been given since it was first awarded in 1937, and acknowledged Jewison as one of the greatest directors and producers of all time. While Jewison has publicly lamented that "marketing has become more important than filmmaking" in Hollywood, his Thalberg award shows that sometimes quality still wins over hype in the industry.

In 1982, Jewison was made a Companion of the Order of Canada, and he also has a star on Canada's Walk of Fame in downtown Toronto.

FIRSTS AND FOREMOSTS IN COMEDY

MACK SENNETT – FOREMOST DIRECTOR OF SLAPSTICK COMEDIES

Born Mikall Sinott in Danville, Quebec, in 1880 to Irish immigrant parents, Mack Sennett would travel through his lifetime from his cold and humble beginnings to the warm climes and riches of the film business in California. Along the way, Sennett revolutionized comedy films.

His family moved to East Berlin, Connecticut, in 1897, and then on to Northampton, Massachusetts. At that time, Sennett was a labourer at American Iron Works, but when he met actress Marie Dressler in 1902 he left for New York to attempt an acting career. However, he soon focused more on screenwriting when he learned that the legendary director D. W. Griffith of Biograph Studios paid twenty-five dollars a script. By 1910, Sennett was also directing, completing two short comedy films each week.

In 1912, he formed the Keystone Production Company with two bookies. Working with the cooperative weather in California, the company finished about 140 short slapstick comedy films in its first year. Legendary performers such as Mabel Normand, "Fatty" Arbuckle, Chester Conklin, and Charlie Chaplin all worked with Sennett over the next few years. Almost all the films centred on a chase scene, often involving the Keystone Kops, but in one film Normand threw a pie at her co-star, and the pie-in-the-face routine soon became another mark of a Sennett film.

In 1914, Sennett directed the first full-length feature comedy film, entitled *Tillie's Punctured Romance* and starring fellow Canadian Marie Dressler, Chaplin, and Normand. By this time, Normand and Sennett were deeply involved. Their romance continued into the 1920s, but she left him because he spent too much time making films. Normand died in 1930, only thirty-three years old and tainted by an earlier investigation of the murder of her boyfriend at the time, director William Taylor, a shooting involving her chauffeur and her gun and rumours of drug addiction.

By that time, silent films were fading and being replaced by the "talkies" and Sennett's career was under similar pressures. In the early 1930s, he produced a few short films featuring W. C. Fields and one with Buster Keaton, and a musical film with Bing Crosby. Soon after, however, Sennett was out of work and poor and so he returned to Canada.

In 1937, Sennett was awarded a special Academy Award for "his lasting contribution to the comedy technique of the screen." He died in 1960 after surgery for kidney problems. Canadian comedian Dan Aykroyd played Sennett in the 1992 feature film *Chaplin*.

WAYNE AND SHUSTER – FOREMOST COMEDIANS
Johnny Wayne and Frank Shuster set an early standard for Canadian comedians to meet when they became enormously popular in Canada, the U.S., and elsewhere. The pair first became popular with their Second World War comedy routine, *The Army Show*. They wrote

and starred in *The Invasion Review,* the first show to play to Allied troops in Normandy after D-Day.

Their CBC television specials were seasonal hits through the decades, and in the U.S. they appeared sixty-seven times on *The Ed Sullivan Show*, the most appearances by any act. Shuster invariably played the straight man to Wayne, whose manic characters included a toga-wearing detective in their classic Julius Caesar murder investigation skit.

Among other awards given to the legendary duo, Frank Shuster was appointed to the Order of Canada in 1997, and in May 1999 Wayne and Shuster had a star dedicated to them on Canada's Walk of Fame in downtown Toronto. Johnny Wayne died in 1990.

SATURDAY NIGHT LIVE – LONGEST RUNNING,
MOST HIGHLY RATED LATE-NIGHT COMEDY SHOW

Saturday Night Live, or SNL as it is known to many people, has not only set records for enduring popularity, it has also launched the careers of many Canadian comedians who have gone on to achieve their own firsts and foremosts in the world.

SNL was the brainchild of Canadian Lorne Michaels. Michaels, born November 17, 1944, in Toronto, started out in television as a producer and performer in the 1960s on the CBC show *The Hart & Lorne Terrific Hour.* With offers of work in hand, Michaels went to the U.S. in the early 1970s and initially was a writer for the Rowan and Martin *Laugh-In* show.

SNL first aired in 1975 and quickly became a high-rated show with such stars as Chevy Chase, John Belushi, Gilda Radner, Jane Curtin, and Bill Murray. Joining the original cast was Canadian Dan Aykroyd. Born on Canada Day, 1952, in Ottawa, Aykroyd would go on from SNL in 1979 to star in over fifty films and TV series, including the Hollywood hits *The Blues Brothers, Ghostbusters,* and *Driving Miss Daisy.* Aykroyd always maintained his connections to Canada, including starring in the CBC-TV special *The Arrow,* the story of the development and dismantling of Canada's Avro Arrow aircraft, which in the late 1950s was considered to be the most advanced military jet ever made.

Michaels has been responsible for recruiting and supporting several other Canadian comedians through SNL over the past twenty-five years. Along the way, he has produced over twenty films and TV series, including the *Wayne's World* films and the *Kids in the Hall* TV show. Among other Canadian comedians who have worked with Michaels, Paul Shaffer did a stint on SNL from 1978 to 1980, and has been the Music Supervisor with the TV show *Late Night with David Letterman* since 1982; Martin Short starred in SNL in 1984–85, then went on to a successful film career; Phil Hartman starred from 1986 to 1994, and also worked for other shows, such as providing the voice of Troy McClure on *The Simpsons,* before his death in 1998; Norm Macdonald played the anchor for the "Weekend Update" news show sketch, among other characters, from 1993 to 1998; Bruce McCulloch worked on SNL in 1985–86 and 1994–95; and fellow *Kids in the Hall* alumnus Mark McKinney worked on the show from 1994 to 1997.

Mike Myers created several characters in addition to Wayne on the show from 1989 to 1994. Born May 25, 1963, in Scarborough, Ontario, Myers went on to create the Austin Powers character for the 1997 surprise hit film *Austin Powers: International Man of Mystery.* The sequel *Austin Powers: The Spy Who Shagged Me* became the the top opening comedy ever, and the top June opening film ever, when it earned $76.6 million in its first three days in theatres in June 1999.

ROY WARD DICKSON
INVENTOR OF THE GAME SHOW

While teaching, Roy Ward Dickson designed a quiz for his students to test their knowledge. He approached several newspapers with the idea of printing the quiz for the public's amusement, but was rejected.

In the early 1930s, Dickson adapted his quiz for radio play, adding prizes that would be given out to those who could answer questions correctly. He called the game *Professor Dick and His Question Box,* and on May 15, 1935, the show was aired for the first time in Toronto.

Dickson had to buy the air time out of his own pocket, and his investment had an unexpected payoff. By 1937 there were more than two hundred quiz shows playing on radio stations across North American.

Another Canadian, Alex Trebek, born July 22, 1940, in Sudbury, Ontario, has reached the pinnacle of game shows, hosting the very popular TV show *Jeopardy!* since 1984. Trebek first hosted a TV game show in 1974, called *The Wizard of Odds*, and he went on to host five other game shows before *Jeopardy!* He has appeared in over thirty TV shows and films, and his role has almost always been as the host of *Jeopardy!* Along the way he has become something of a North American icon.

HUGH LE CAINE
INVENTOR OF THE ELECTRONIC SYNTHESIZER AND MULTI-TRACK RECORDER

While Casavant Frères Ltd. was becoming the world's foremost organ manufacturer (see story above), and Frank Morse Robb of Belleville, Ontario, was introducing the first electronic wave organ to the world in the late 1920s (see story in *Canada Firsts*), another Canadian, Hugh Le Caine, was exploring his interest in electronic music at high school in his hometown of Port Arthur (now Thunder Bay). Le Caine, born in 1914, would himself go on to make several contributions to the electronic music field, especially with keyboards.

After high school, Le Caine spent a year studying piano in Toronto, and then began a degree in engineering and physics at Queen's University in Kingston, Ontario. By the time he finished in 1939, he had already built his first electronic instrument, a reed organ, and adapted part of the organ for use as an electrometer, which became a standard instrument for measuring ionization in laboratories worldwide.

He joined the National Research Council (NRC) after graduation, working in the field of radar development throughout the war years.

His work on electronic instruments was somewhat on the back burner, although he continued to explore developments in his home studio. In fact, it would not be until 1954 that Le Caine would be allowed to work at the NRC on his musical inventions, as they were not viewed as priority research areas. Another reason his work in this area was postponed was that Le Caine was busy with doctoral studies in nuclear physics at Birmingham University in England from 1948 to 1952.

Before this, however, in 1945, Le Caine invented an electronic synthesizer keyboard he called the Sackbut, after a medieval instrument that was the forerunner of the trombone. The name in part described the ability of Le Caine's instrument to slide from note to note, while also changing tone, colour, and pitch simply by touching the keys in different ways. The "touch-sensitive" keyboard of the Sackbut allowed the instrument to imitate many other instruments with varying tonal qualities. Le Caine also developed a Touch Sensitive Organ (TSO) between 1945 and 1953 using the same technology, which solved the problem of keys clicking each time notes changed in a song.

After the 1955 Canadian Trade Fair, the Baldwin Organ Company bought a long-term option on the TSO, but never produced it for sale. It is suspected that Baldwin simply wanted to control the technology, as they developed a key design that did not click several years later, and incorporated it into their line of organs.

Meanwhile, Le Caine's Sackbut preceded Robert Moog's claimed invention of the synthesizer by nineteen years. Regrettably, Le Caine's achievement has been overlooked because when he invented the Sackbut there was no commercial market for synthesizers. In the early 1970s, the NRC unfortunately awarded a licence to manufacture the Sackbut to an inexperienced company and several years later no instruments had been produced.

In 1955, Le Caine began working on a multiple-tape tape recorder, and came up with the most flexible tape-recording mechanism ever built. The recorder could play ten stereo tapes simultaneously, and the speed and volume of each tape could be changed at any time.

Using this invention, Le Caine wrote many compositions, including "Dripsody," based on the sound of a single drop of water. Unlike the Sackbut, the Multi-track (known formally as the Special Purpose Tape Recorder) soon became well known worldwide, although it was never licensed for mass production.

Finally, Le Caine also developed the Paramus Music System in the early 1970s, a method of controlling the sound generators in synthesizers using computers. His system became the standard in the design of synthesizers several years later.

In recognition of his achievements, including four patents for his inventions, Le Caine received honorary doctorates from Queen's University, the University of Toronto, and McGill University. Le Caine retired from the NRC in 1976, and died prematurely in 1977 at age sixty-three, unfortunately largely unknown as a true pioneer in musical innovations.

FIRST AND FOREMOSTS IN POPULAR MUSIC

Canadians have made their mark on popular music for decades through such recording stars as Paul Anka, Joni Mitchell, Neil Young, The Band, Gordon Lightfoot, The Guess Who, Leonard Cohen, Ian and Sylvia Tyson, and R. Dean Taylor (who both co-wrote million-selling songs for The Supremes and also recorded the million-selling *Indiana Wants Me* for Motown Records' Rare Earth label). While these artists did not achieve clear firsts or foremosts in the world, they and others set the stage, so to speak, for Canadian singers and songwriters who in the past decade have become popular worldwide, often with the help of producer David Foster.

Formerly of British Columbia, Foster has been nominated for a Grammy by the National Academy of Recording Arts and Sciences thirty times since 1979, has won fourteen times, and was also awarded a President's Merit award in 1998. Other Canadian Grammy winners include Percy Faith for record of the year in 1960; Gale Garnett, for best folk performance in 1964; Anne Murray, who won her first award in 1974 and has won a few times since then; and pianist Oscar Peterson, who has won several times for various jazz recordings, including awards in 1977, 1978, and 1979.

At the 1998 Grammy Awards, four Canadian female singer/songwriters were nominated for an unprecedented twenty-seven awards. The firsts and foremosts these and other Canadian music artists have achieved in popular music are set out below.

THE CREW-CUTS – WORLD'S FIRST ROCK-AND-ROLL HIT

In the early 1950s, rock and roll was just beginning to break through as popular music. In no small part, it was held back by discrimination against black artists such as Fats Domino and Johnny Otis who were the pioneers of the music.

One black band, the Chords, recorded their song "Sh-Boom," but it did not get wide airplay. A Canadian quartet called the Crew-Cuts and made up of Rudi Maugeri, Pat Barrett, John Perkins, and his brother Ray were playing around Ontario at the time. The four members were well trained, having sung in the choir at Toronto's St. Michael's Cathedral.

Eventually, the Crew-Cuts were offered a chance to record in New York, and their version of "Sh-Boom" became a number-one hit, what many consider to be the first rock and roll hit. The members of the group acknowledge that they were reaping the benefits of doing covers of other groups' songs, but also maintain that in the U.S. at the time it was the only way that the music could have broken through the race barrier.

In 1984, the Crew-Cuts were named to the Canadian Music Hall of Fame.

BUFFY SAINTE-MARIE – FOREMOST ABORIGINAL ARTIST AND UNITED NATIONS SPOKESPERSON

Buffy Sainte-Marie's mother was of the Cree band, which is part of the Algonquian family of aboriginal people, the largest aboriginal group in Canada. Sainte-Marie was born February 20, 1941, on the Piapot Reserve in Saskatchewan, but was later adopted and raised in Maine.

Sainte-Marie would go on to write several protest and love songs that became classics in the 1960s, and were recorded by other artists such as Barbra Streisand, Elvis Presley, Neil Diamond, and Janis Joplin. One of her best known songs is "Universal Soldier" from her debut album *It's My Way.*

Sainte-Marie released twelve more albums, including two "best of" compilations, before leaving the industry in 1976 to raise her son and study experimental music. In 1982, she won an Academy Award for writing the theme song for the film *An Officer and a Gentleman* entitled "Up Where We Belong."

Sainte-Marie returned to recording, releasing the album *Coincidence and Unlikely Stories.* That year she was named best international artist by France, was chosen by the United Nations to proclaim the International Year of Indigenous People, and helped create a new Juno Awards category for aboriginal music.

Her most recent album, released in 1996, was entitled *Up Here Where We Belong.* Among many other awards, Sainte-Marie has been recognized with a star on Canada's Walk of Fame in downtown Toronto.

BRYAN ADAMS – WORLD'S MOST SUCCESSFUL ROCK SINGLE

Bryan Adams was born November 5, 1959, in Kingston, Ontario, and grew up in Ottawa. Too young to experience the blossoming of popular rock music in the 1960s, he came of age in the super-group era of the 1970s.

By the winter of 1979, Adams had spent some time as the lead singer of the group Sweeney Todd, when he was only sixteen, and recorded a minor disco hit, "Let Me Take You Dancin'." He had formed a songwriting partnership with Jim Vallance of the group Prism in 1976, and was pushing high-profile manager Bruce Allen to sign him up. Allen gave him a break, and since then Adams has fulfilled his promise that he would be the biggest artist Allen would ever manage.

Through his youth, and into his own career, popular music has grown enormously, with artists enjoying international success more and more often as portable radios have become widely available and radio airplay has helped promote songs quickly around the world.

In 1991, these factors along with his dedication and years of hard work building his career no doubt helped Adams when he released what soon became the most popular rock song ever, entitled "Everything I Do (I Do It For You)." The song was number one in the United Kingdom for sixteen weeks, and number one in the U.S. for seven weeks, and won a Grammy Award that year for Best Song Specifically Written for a Motion Picture or Television.

Adams has sold an estimated 50,000,000 albums worldwide, and in 1992 he was given a Special Recognition Award (Juno) for Unprecedented Global Success for his record-breaking song by the Canadian Academy of Recording Arts and Sciences. He has won six other Juno awards, along with many awards in the U.S., the United Kingdom, Germany, Austria, Japan, and Australia. Adams is also immortalized on Canada's Walk of Fame in downtown Toronto.

Adams has also donated his time to the cause of finding a cure for breast cancer, helping Canadian supermodel Linda Evangelista raise about $800,000 during a benefit in Ontario in early 1999. Adams has spent much of his career based in Vancouver, B.C., but he now lives in London, England.

CÉLINE DION – FOREMOST FEMALE POP VOCALIST

The youngest of fourteen children, Dion was born March 30, 1968, in the small town of Charlemagne, Quebec. At age five, she made her singing debut at the restaurant-bar owned by her parents. Seven years later, her demo tape caused Réné Angelil to mortgage his house to raise funds to produce her first album, released in 1981.

Through the 1980s, Dion released another eight albums and played to sold-out audiences in Quebec and elsewhere, including to 65,000 fans and Pope John Paul II at a concert in 1984. Through these years, and with Angelil as her manager, Dion won fifteen Felix Awards (the

Quebec version of the Juno Award), and in 1988 she won first prize at the Eurovision Song Contest held in Dublin, Ireland, and performed her winning song for six hundred million television viewers worldwide at the awards ceremony. She also became the first Canadian singer to have a platinum record in France when she sold more than 700,000 copies of her single "D'amour ou d'amitie."

Dion's album *Unison,* released in 1990, was her first English recording, and it won two Juno Awards. Her five-octave range and ability to sing in both French and English have given her a wide-ranging global audience, and as a result she has become one of the most-awarded and best-known pop artists of all time.

In 1991 Dion had two songs nominated for a Grammy. She won her first Grammy for her number-one-selling title song from Disney's movie *Beauty and the Beast.* In 1992 she won another ten awards at various ceremonies. She became the top-selling female recording artist of all time in 1993 with the release of her album *The Colour of My Love,* which included the million-selling single "Think Twice." The album was number one on the British charts for five weeks and the single for seven weeks, a record unbroken since The Beatles held the position with the album and single *Help!* in 1965. Dion also released a French language album that year, *D'eux,* that sold ten million copies in the first twelve months and became the top-selling French language album of all time.

In 1994, Dion and Angelil were married. Two years later, her album *Falling Into You* was released and it would go on to sell more than twenty-five million copies, become number one on the charts in eleven countries, and win the Grammy awards for Best Pop Album and Album of the Year. The same production team, including David Foster, helped Dion put out the album *Let's Talk About Love* only one year later, which included the Academy Award- and Grammy-winning theme song "My Heart Will Go On" from the film *Titanic,* and which sold over twenty-five million copies.

As of spring 1999, Dion had won 110 career awards including five Grammy awards, three World Music Awards, 19 Juno awards, and 33 Felix awards. While accepting yet another award at the 1999 Juno

Award ceremony, Dion announced that she was going to take a break from performing.

Dion was appointed to the Order of Canada in May 1998. She is the spokeswoman for the Canadian Cystic Fibrosis Foundation, a position she holds in memory of her niece who died of the disease.

ALANIS MORISSETTE – WORLD'S BEST-SELLING ALBUM BY A FEMALE SOLO ARTIST

Alanis Morissette is another female Canadian singer whose career began when she was quite young. Born in Ottawa on June 1, 1974, Morissette recorded herself at age nine singing covers of songs and original compositions on a tape cassette and sent it to friends of her parents, Lindsay and Jacqui Morgan, who had toured as folksingers in the 1970s and into the 1980s. Morissette's parents and their friends supported her as she pursued her career, but she had difficulty at first securing a recording contract, mainly because she was so young. Along with Lindsay Morgan and other local producers in Ottawa, Morissette produced demo tapes and videos and performed locally through the late 1980s until, finally, she signed with MCA in Canada. In April 1991, they released her first album, *Alanis,* which was a huge success. That year she won the Juno Award for best new female vocalist.

After a second album did not sell very well, Morissette moved to Toronto in June 1993 at the urging of her new Los Angeles-based manager. She began working with other songwriters, about one hundred in total, and completed dozens of songs. She was searching for an artistic identity, and in some circles was criticized because she was exploring all sorts of melodies and styles very different from the dance style of her early records.

In 1995, Morissette remade herself, and her career, when she released the album *Jagged Little Pill.* Morissette wrote and recorded the album with Los Angeles-based musician and producer Glen Ballard. Ballard had worked with a wide range of major artists in the past, including Quincy Jones, Aretha Franklin, Michael Jackson,

Natalie Cole, and Barbra Streisand, playing on, producing, or writing albums that have sold nearly one hundred million copies. Together, he and Morissette created what some commentators view as the first album of a new genre of young, angry, female rock-and-roll singers.

In any case, the album became the best-selling album ever by a female solo artist, and won four Grammy awards that year, including Best Rock Album and Album of the Year. As of May 1999, over twenty-eight million copies of *Jagged Little Pill* had been sold, including sixteen million in the U.S. It is the first album by a Canadian artist that has ever sold over two million copies in Canada. In 1997, the album was named favourite pop rock album at the American Music Awards, and Morissette was awarded a special Juno for international achievement.

Morissette's second album, *Supposed Former Infatuation Junkie,* set the record for best-selling record for the first week of its 1998 release when three million copies were sold. That year, she won two Grammy awards for her song "Uninvited." On June 25, 1999, Morissette achieved another first when the video for her song "So Pure" from the album became the first video by a major artist to be released on the Internet instead of television.

SHANIA TWAIN – WORLD'S BEST-SELLING FEMALE COUNTRY-MUSIC ARTIST AND ALBUM

Shania Twain was born Eilleen Regina Edwards on August 28, 1965, in Windsor, Ontario. Her parents separated when she was two years old, and her mother moved the family to Timmins, Ontario. When she was six, Twain was officially adopted by her mother's new husband, Jerry Twain. Her new father was a native Canadian of the Ojibwa band, and he and her mother changed her name to Shania, which means "I'm on my way" in the Ojibwa language.

Twain sang from a young age on, earning a bit of extra money for the family to help raise her many siblings. Her parents played mostly country music records at home, but Twain also listened to Motown and folk artists. In 1986, tragically, her parents were killed in a car accident, and Twain took on responsibility for her teenage brothers and sisters. She eventually secured a full-time job performing at the Deerhurst Resort in Huntsville, Ontario.

In 1993, she recorded her first album, self-titled, and from there her popularity began to grow. She broke through in world-record style in 1995 with the world's best-selling country music album ever for a female artist, entitled *The Woman in Me,* and it made her the best-selling female country-music artist ever. Twain co-wrote all of the songs on the album with her producer Robert John (Mutt) Lange, who had also produced records for Canadian Bryan Adams, Def Leppard, and AC/DC. Twain and Lange were married in 1994.

In the summer of 1996, Timmins changed the name of its main street to Shania Twain Way, and presented her with the first-ever key to the city. In 1997, Twain released the album *Come on Over,* which has sold six-and-a-half million copies worldwide, and she was named favourite female country artist at the American Music Awards. That year, she was also awarded a special Juno Award for International Achievement. In 1999, Twain and Lange won two Grammy Awards for their song "You're Still the One."

Twain and Lange currently live in upstate New York but plan to move to Switzerland to escape some of the media attention that follows them everywhere in North America.

SARAH McLACHLAN – CREATED FIRST AND LARGEST ALL-FEMALE MUSIC FESTIVAL

While thousands of music festivals have taken place over the decades, before the summer of 1996 not one had focused solely on female musicians. That year, Canadian singer and songwriter Sarah McLachlan took her idea on the road, and the Lilith Fair was born. The Fair is coordinated by McLachlan, Terry McBride and Dan Fraser of Nettwerk Productions, who manage and produce McLachlan's albums, and her New York-based agent Marty Diamond.

In 1997, the tour grew to include thirty-five concerts spread over seven weeks, and was the top-grossing festival of the year with gross

revenues of about $23 million. Extensive international media cover-
age almost turned the festival into a movement with a message that
year. McLachlan sold five million albums worldwide through the year
and also won two awards at the 1998 Grammy Awards for her songs
"Building a Mystery" and "Last Dance" and four awards at the 1998
Juno Awards.

In the summer of 1998, the festival tour made an incredible fifty-
seven stops in North America over twelve weeks, and was again the
top-grossing festival with revenues of more than $44 million (includ-
ing raising about $2 million for various charities). The festival also
travelled at other times that year to England and Australia for
concerts. Major female recording artists such as Sinead O'Connor,
Natalie Merchant, Tracy Chapman, Indigo Girls, Erykah Badu, and
Sheryl Crow, among others, appeared at the concerts.

In the summer of 1999, the final year of the Fair, McLachlan and
her colleagues scaled back touring to forty concerts over seven-
and-a-half weeks in order to lessen the burden of coordinating the
festival.

FIRSTS AND FOREMOSTS IN COMPUTER ANIMATION

Canadians have been at the forefront of computer animation since its
very beginnings, as the following sections detail.

NESTOR BURTNYK – INVENTOR OF COMPUTER ANIMATION PROGRAMS

Nestor Burtnyk was born in 1929 near Dauphin, Manitoba, before
computers and television had been invented, and soon after silent
movies had been displaced by the "talkies." He grew up without a real
vision of what he wanted to do for a career, and perhaps wouldn't
have studied beyond high school if he hadn't received a scholarship to
attend the University of Manitoba in Winnipeg.

Burtnyk studied electrical engineering because his older brother Victor had done so, and he followed him to Ottawa after graduating in 1950. From this unlikely start, Burtnyk would go on to revolutionize the production of animation with computer programs.

He obtained a job as a junior research officer at the National Research Council (NRC) on the advice of a former professor, and initially was assigned to defence research. However, in 1967 Burtnyk and his colleagues began to investigate computer graphics. Using the rudimentary computer equipment available at the time, Burtnyk developed a computer program and work station that allowed him to design images and move them using a menu-driven screen and a computer mouse (the second ever created) made of mahogany.

As he learned more about animation through conferences and animators, Burtnyk focused more directly on mechanizing the process. In the early 1970s, he developed a program that could fill in the blanks between the still frames that depict key actions in any cartoon by entering computer code. It was the first, key step to computerizing the traditional method of painting thousands of frames by hand to link two action frames.

The NRC approached the National Film Board with the technology, and by 1974 their joint efforts produced the ten-minute film *La Faim/Hunger*. Drawn by French animator Peter Foldes, and based on a shorter film called *Metadata*, the film portrayed the disparity of wealth between rich and poor countries. It won the Prix du jury at the Cannes Film Festival, and became the first computer-animated film to be nominated for an Academy Award.

Burtnyk and his NRC colleagues, especially Marceli Wein, went on to develop other computer animation techniques, all of which form the basis of the advanced animation now shown more and more on television and film screens around the world. In 1996, Burtnyk and Wein were awarded a special Academy Award for their inventions and developments in computer animation.

FOREMOST COMPUTER ANIMATION SCHOOLS AND COMPANIES

The world-leading work of Burtnyk and Wein has been continued by several Canadian schools and companies. Sheridan College in Oakville, Ontario, is considered to be the "Harvard" of computer animation and graphics schools, its reputation attributed to the founder and chair of the program, Robin King. The Sheridan College program was set up in 1980. Courses at the University of Toronto, the University of Montreal, and the University of Waterloo are also highly regarded.

Other Canadians have set up their own companies with great success. An early world leader in the field through the 1980s was Omnibus, based in Toronto with connections to the NRC and the NFB's pioneering work. However, Omnibus made a crucial error when it invested in mainframe computers, while other companies used low-cost personal computers.

Since then, Toronto-based companies Side Effects (co-founded by Kim Davidson who worked at Omnibus) and Alias Research (which was bought by Silicon Technologies in 1995 and then combined with Wavefront Technologies), and Montreal-based Discreet Logic and Softimage (sold to Avid Technology Inc. in 1998) have led several other companies in Canada that design special effects software. These four companies dominate the $6-billion-a-year industry in North America.

Each of the companies has developed its own software to create specific effects, such as the Prisms and Houdini programs from Side Effects; Flame, Flint, and Inferno from Discreet Logic; 3D by Softimage; PowerAnimator from Alias, and its replacement called Maya from Alias–Wavefront. Side Effects and Alias–Wavefront are known for three-dimensional modelling; Softimage's products are often used to animate objects; and Discreet Logic's software has been widely used to colour and give texture to objects, and to create depth and mimic the look of scenes shot with cameras so that special effects don't look out of place in a film.

These companies' products have been used to create various

Academy Award-winning effects in many feature films, including *Titanic, Godzilla, The X-Files, True Lies, The Flintstones, Toy Story,* Canadian director Atom Egoyan's *The Sweet Hereafter,* and *The Mask* (which starred Canadian Jim Carrey), along with television shows such as *TekWars, The Outer Limits,* and commercials for Sugar Crisp, Oreo cookies, Lifesavers, and Coke commercials in Mexico.

C.O.R.E. Digital Pictures, another Toronto-based company, set up by Canadian William Shatner of *Star Trek* fame, has created special effects scenes for the feature film *Johnny Mnemonic,* which starred Canadian Keanu Reeves, and *Dr. Doolittle,* among others. Another computer animation film with Canadian connections is *Spawn,* released in 1997. The character Spawn, a sort of anti-hero, was created by Calgary artist Todd McFarlane after he led a walkout at Marvel Comics in the late 1980s. He and six other artists started up Image Comics, now the third-largest publisher of comics. The film version of *Spawn* featured computer animation by George Lucas's industry-leading company, Industrial Light and Magic, which employs seventy Canadians, all graduates of the Sheridan College program. McFarlane has also started his own toy company to produce Spawn-related toys, among others, and Spawn video games and a cable TV show have also been produced. For example, the toy company produced Austin Power toys based on the popular film character created by Canadian comedian Mike Myers (see "Firsts and foremosts in comedy" above).

Another pioneering Canadian company in a different area of the film industry has also produced recent innovations in the area of animation. As detailed in *Canada Firsts,* IMAX cameras to make big-screen films and the theatres to show them were invented by Canadians in the late 1960s, and have gone on to dominate this part of the film industry. By 1994, Imax Corporation of Mississauga, Ontario, had produced over twenty films, mostly documentaries, and helped open one hundred theatres. That year, the company was taken over by American investment bankers Brad Wechsler and Richard Gelfond, with help from the takeover specialist firm Wasserstein Perella & Co.

Under the new management, Imax has produced more films, opened more theatres, and entered into the new area of three-dimensional films including inventing a 3-D animation technique called Stereo Animation Drawing Device (SANDDE). *Paint Misbehavin'*, which debuted in 1997, was the first animated short film made using the technique. While 2-D IMAX films such as the independently produced 1998 feature *Everest* have brought more people into IMAX theatres than ever before (the film is expected to gross more than $100 million in its first two years), Imax is hoping that the 3-D format will also increase interest in IMAX films. As of early 1999, Imax had four 3-D films in production, including 3-D animation films *Cyberworld* and *Gulliver's Travels*.

REBOOT – FIRST COMPUTER ANIMATION TELEVISION SERIES

Another Canadian company has created the first computer animation TV series. In 1991, Steve Barron, film director and head of Limelight Productions, brought together Chris Brough, who had worked for twenty years as a writer and producer in Los Angeles, and the London, England-based commercial animation outfit called The Hub and made up of Ian Pearson, Phil Mitchell, and Gavin Blair. Pearson had registered a first in the world already when he created computer-animated characters for the video for the Dire Straits' song "Money for Nothing." American-born Brough and The Hub brainstormed the idea of the TV series, and they all moved to Vancouver, where Brough had done a lot of work since 1986.

Working out of a room at the Granville Island Hotel, the quartet, now called Mainframe Entertainment Inc., developed short clips of the TV series on a couple of computers and tried to sell the series based on the demo tapes to the ABC, YTV, and ITV television networks. At that time, computer animation longer than a few minutes had never been created, so the networks were sceptical that it could be done. They had good reason, if they only had known, to be cautious. When ABC wanted to examine Mainframe's operations more closely on short notice, the quartet was forced to set up an office in thirty-six hours to make it appear that they were an established company.

Their efforts paid off as ABC signed on, and further financial support came soon after from Alliance Communications and Polygram Video. Mainframe worked for over a year solving software problems, creating characters, and developing stock character and background images for repeated use. Their efforts to finish shows in time to meet the broadcast schedule were aided by the new R4000 chip for use with Silicon Graphics computers, which increased the speed of creating images by 50 per cent.

Between 1994 and 1998, three seasons of the series, called *ReBoot,* were created and broadcast. The half-hour show follows the adventures of the hero Matrix and his colleagues as they explore the Net, the Web, and the real world. The show's thirty-nine episodes have been aired on various networks in over seventy countries.

Beginning with fifteen people, and now employing over 240 software programmers, designers, animators, and administrative staff, Mainframe has created, amazingly, over 1,800 minutes of computer animation. Beyond *ReBoot,* Mainframe also developed the show *Beast Wars–Transformers* (called *Beasties* in Canada) with the Hasbro Toy Group and YTV Canada. The show, aired for the past three years in over thirty countries, is based upon Transformer toys, which can be changed from animal to robot form. Another show, called *War Planets* (*Shadow Raiders* in Canada), was launched in September 1998, while *Weird-Ohs* began airing in January 1999. As well, Mainframe has produced *ReBoot* as a video game and two *ReBoot* films for use in IMAX amusement rides, the first of which was released in October 1997 and won the award for best new product from the International Association of Amusement Parks and Attractions. Mainframe is now working on its first feature-length computer animation film.

To produce these shows, Mainframe has used basic animating software from Softimage, but has also had to develop new software, such as the Grin program for lip-synching. Mainframe's efforts have garnered several awards, including four Gemini awards from the Canadian industry association, and an Emmy for production design from the U.S. television association. In addition, examples of its work were added to the Innovation Collection at the Smithsonian Institute in 1998.

While computer animation software is still limited in many ways, unable yet to create lifelike humans that can be viewed up close, or hair that adequately depicts the diversity of texture and colour of the real thing, the programs have been used to create amazingly realistic effects, especially in fast-moving films. No matter how the industry develops in the future, it seems certain that Canadians will be involved in many further innovations, given their achievements to date in this relatively new art form.

INVENTION AND DEVELOPMENT OF GYRO-STABILIZED CAMERA SYSTEM

If you have ever tried to use your video camera to capture your boating, helicopter, or car trip, then you would appreciate the camera technology developed by Wescam Inc. Wescam's cameras take jitter-free images on the most rocking and rolling of rides, and are world leaders in the field. Newer home-video cameras can stabilize images, but they use electronic equipment to do so, while Wescam's cameras are stabilized by gyroscopes, a more effective system for rotating the camera to capture a clear, stable image.

The Wescam technology was invented by engineer Noxon Leavitt in the late 1960s while he was working in the military division of Westinghouse Canada. Leavitt was born in Prince Edward County, Ontario, and grew up and was educated near Frankfurt, Ontario. The technology was originally developed for battlefield observation, but in 1974 Leavitt bought the equipment and patents from Westinghouse and set up Istec Ltd. to adapt the technology for non-military uses. Although Istec Ltd. was successful in selling stabilized camera systems to television and film companies and government and military operations in numerous countries, the company did not grow to the potential of its products.

In 1985, Mark Chamberlain joined Istec Ltd., and in February 1987 he became co-owner. Chamberlain, born in Toronto, grew up and was educated in Lindsay, Ontario, and then went on to obtain an undergraduate degree in science and a master's in mechanical engineering at the University of Waterloo. Under his direction, Istec began to grow, from $1 million in sales and seventeen employees in 1987 to $12.3 million in sales and sixty employees in 1993. In 1994, the company changed names to Wescam Inc., and the following year entered into an amalgamation with Jefferson Partners Capital Corporation. In the fall of 1995, the company went public, selling $27 million worth of shares. The company now employs 392 people at its headquarters on Innovation Drive in Flamborough, Ontario, and in offices in the U.S., and has distributors in seven other countries. Sales revenues in 1998 were $79.9 million with sales to date in thirty countries around the world.

Throughout this period of expansion, Wescam's products have become much used and much awarded. Another important part of the system is a microwave communications system that can transmit high-quality video and audio from the camera location to a remote viewer. The cameras and other technology have been used in over 130 major motion pictures including: *Star Wars*, *Superman*, *Apollo 13*, *Braveheart*, *Blues Brothers 2000*, *Golden Eye*, *Titanic*, *Armageddon*, and *Fly Away Home* (about Bill Lishman; see "First person to fly with and lead a migration of a flock of birds" in the *Environment* chapter above). In 1990, Wescam won an Academy Award for "significant scientific and technological contribution to the art of filmmaking."

Wescam's products have also helped provide sports coverage of the winter and summer Olympic games between 1992 and 1998 (including Donovan Bailey's 1996 world-record 100-metre win; see *Sport* chapter below for his story), the World Series from 1987 to 1998, Super Bowls, PGA Golf, the 1992 and 1995 America's Cup, and many motor sports events. Since 1987, the company has won sixteen Emmys for its sports coverage, engineering achievements, and other television shows. In addition, the cameras have been used to film commercials for over eighty companies, including most automobile manufacturers, airlines, and a wide assortment of others.

Wescam's equipment is also used for news gathering (the equipment was on four helicopters that filmed O. J. Simpson as his infamous white Ford Bronco was being chased by police down a California highway in 1993), and police and military units also use the cameras for surveillance.

BUSINESS

P.L. ROBERTSON
INVENTOR OF SQUARE-HEAD SCREW AND SCREWDRIVER

Peter Lymburner (P. L.) Robertson invented square-head screws and the Robertson screwdriver to drive them in 1908 in Milton, Ontario. The square-head screw is the best screw in terms of resisting "cam-out," which is the tendency for the screwdriver to slide out of the head of the screw, often damaging the screw, the screwdriver, the work surface, and fingers in the process. As a result, the screwdriver grips a square-head screw better, allowing more force to be used and easier driving.

At the time of his invention, the slot-head screwdriver was in use, and it was, and remains, very prone to camming out (the Phillips screw and screwdriver, with a star-shaped head, were not invented until 1936 by Henry J. Phillips).

The Steel Company of Canada, Robertson's competition, attacked his invention and tried to invalidate his patents. In 1910, *Saturday Night* magazine published an exaggerated story also attacking the invention, to which Robertson responded with a one-thousand-word letter to the editor. In typical Canadian fashion, Robertson had to struggle to find financial support to manufacture the screw. Eventually he succeeded, after resisting an offer from Henry Ford to sell his patent rights (still, some Model A Fords were assembled using square-head screws).

Robertson founded Recess Screws Ltd. in England, and built a plant in Milton that by the end of the Second World War had five hundred employees (it now operates as Robertson-Whithouse and employs about two hundred people). His invention has been used widely in manufacturing and has become a worldwide standard. Robertson died in 1951 at the age of seventy-two, a millionaire, world industrialist, and philanthropist.

FIRSTS AND FOREMOSTS IN MINERAL EXPLORATION

Exploring for mineral deposits has become more and more refined since the days when an accidental discovery of a nugget of gold could spur thousands of people to rush to an area of the world, as happened in the late 1800s in northern Canada. Initially, exploration involved walking the land, then building trails and roads across vast tracts of countryside, and soon after, especially in large countries like Canada, flying over huge territories searching for signs of deposits.

Geobotanists in Russia first developed the techniques of surveying from biplanes for specific types of plants that flourished in part because of deposits of certain minerals in the surface soil. Then, geochemists at the British Geological Survey discovered chemical trace indicators in the deposits' surface soil, and developed detectors that could be carried to the site to analyze soil samples. Later, more sophisticated equipment was developed and attached to planes, helicopters, and ground vehicles to collect and analyze micro-samples of the surface of the earth. Canada's vast ice-, snow-, and lake-covered landscape was a key motivator for these inventions. Mineral exploration on foot or in trucks had proven to be enormously time-consuming and difficult, if not impossible, in many areas of the country.

While all of the more than ninety people in the Canadian Mining Hall of Fame have made leading contributions to Canada's mining industry, five stand out as having achieved firsts or foremosts in the world in these and other mining exploration techniques.

JOSEPH TYRRELL

Joseph Tyrrell has been described as the father of them all because, as Canada's senior geologist in the late 1800s, he was both the last map-making explorer in the country and the first of the modern prospectors. While surveying the Badlands in Alberta in 1884 he discovered fossils of the Albertosaurus (see "Discovery of the Albertosaurus at world's foremost dinosaur fossil site" in the *Science* chapter above). In 1893, he and his team completed the first survey, by canoe, dog sled, and snowshoe, of much of the thousands of kilometres of so-called Barren Lands from Lake Athabasca (straddling the border of northern Alberta and Saskatchewan) to Hudson Bay.

In addition, Mary Tyrrell, Joseph's spouse, was the founder and first president of the Women's Association of the Mining Industry of Canada in 1921. The association provides scholarships for earth science students and other support for the industry.

WILLET GREEN MILLER

Willet Green Miller was born in 1866, and went on to graduate from the University of Toronto in 1890 in natural science. He continued his education at Harvard, Chicago, and Heidelberg universities, while spending summers mapping for the Canadian Geological Survey. In 1902, Miller became the first provincial geologist for the province of Ontario, and he made many contributions to the mining industry in this role.

Among his achievements, Miller discovered a method to identify diamonds, emeralds, corundum, and emery using X-rays. This method was used in prospecting for commodities such as corundum, an abrasive, and resulted in Ontario supplying 82 per cent of the world's corundum in 1906. When samples of ore were sent to him from staked land in Cobalt, Ontario, he corrected the prospectors' mistaken belief that they had found copper. In fact, the sample contained nickel and cobalt, and during a follow-up expedition Miller found silver. His discoveries led to the first precious-metal mines in Ontario. For his work, Miller received, fittingly, the gold medal of the Institute of Mining and Metallurgy of London in 1915.

C. STANLEY DAVIDSON

C. Stanley Davidson, born in Montreal in 1900, took automated mineral exploration into the air. After receiving his master's in science in 1925 (he was awarded a Ph.D. from Harvard later in life), Davidson worked as mine surveyor, field engineer, and chief geologist at various mining sites. He ended up working with Inco in Sudbury, and there in the early 1940s he put together an electromagnetic device with the help of a mine technician, and based on a description in a textbook.

When he tested and refined his new device, Davidson found that it could distinguish between different types of metals in deposits in the ground. Several ore deposits in the Sudbury area were found using the equipment. Later, Davidson developed a mobile unit that could be pulled by snowmobiles or tractors, and then developed the first operational airborne electromagnetic system ever constructed. This unit was used by Inco to discover the Heath Steele copper-lead-zinc deposit in New Brunswick and the Thompson nickel ore body in Manitoba. Davidson died in 1967, but his technique of airborne surveying is still in use around the world.

HAROLD SEIGEL

Harold Seigel also developed several mining exploration techniques. Born in Toronto, Ontario, in 1924, Seigel obtained his Ph.D. in geophysics from the University of Toronto in 1949. The focus of his doctoral thesis was on the pioneering development of the Induced Polarization method for exploration. He formed a consulting business in 1956, and in addition to conceiving of Induced Polarization, he also developed the Time-Resolved Photoluminescence method, and was closely involved in the development of about six other geophysical exploration methods. Seigel has been granted twenty-one patents in six countries for his discoveries.

In 1967, Seigel started up Scintrex to produce his equipment, and it and his efforts led to the discovery of about nine mines in Canada and overseas. Seigel retired from the company in 1993, and in 1998 Scintrex was taken over by Intelligent Detection Systems (see "Development of micro-detection equipment" in the *Science* chapter). In recognition of his achievements, Seigel was awarded the J. Tuzo Wilson Medal of the Canadian Geophysical Union in 1985, the Distinguished Service Award of the Prospectors and Developers Association of Canada in 1986, and the A. O. Dufresne Award of the Canadian Institute of Mining in 1987.

ANTHONY BARRINGER

As noted above in "Development of micro-detection equipment" in the *Science* chapter, English-born Anthony Barringer served in the British army during the Second World War, and then returned to university, eventually obtaining his Ph.D. in economic geology from Imperial College in 1954. Hired by Selection Trust Mining Group, a large British mining conglomerate, Barringer was sent to Canada to prospect for minerals with Selco Exploration. He soon became manager of the company's Airborne and Technical Services division.

While in Canada, Barringer began to develop what came to be called the INPUT (Induced Pulse Transient) airborne electromagnetic (EM) system for exploration. Barringer's new INPUT technology soon became the foremost fixed-wing airborne survey system and has been used to discover more than twenty-five commercial ore deposits with a combined value of over $60 billion.

In 1961, he formed Barringer Research Ltd., a private company based in Toronto. As a result of lack of financial support for high technology companies in Canada (still an ongoing problem), Barringer listed his company on the NASDAQ stock exchange in 1967 to raise funds to develop further products and services for the industry.

In addition to the INPUT system, Barringer developed several other geophysical and geochemical analyzers for mineral exploration such as FLUOROSCAN, used for oil and gas exploration, and holds about fifty patents in this and other areas. Some of Barringer's exploration innovations have found other uses, such as GASPEC, an infrared remote sensor for atmospheric gases which has been used by NASA to measure the worldwide atmospheric distribution of carbon dioxide. Also, he used INPUT's metal-detecting system to invent metal detectors that prevent errant pieces of metal from getting caught in and wrecking ore crushers by triggering a halt of the conveyor belt carrying the ore. He also invented the walk-through metal detector that is now used in airports and other locations worldwide.

Other applications of his inventions include searching for sunken treasure in the ocean, and optical sensors he developed measure increases in sulphur dioxide emissions (which indicate the temperature is rising) in volcanos around the world.

Since 1977 Barringer has lived in Denver, Colorado, and he has been a citizen of the United States for several years. He retired in 1989, but has remained active and engaged with several research laboratories in the U.S. He has received many awards and honours throughout his career, including the Logan Medal of the Geological Association of Canada and the Jackling Award of the American Association of Mining and Petroleum Engineers.

FIRSTS AND FOREMOSTS IN MINING AND REFINERY OPERATIONS

In addition to the five leaders in mineral exploration, the Canadian Mining Hall of Fame includes ten people who have led the world in mining and refinery operations. In many cases, mining and refinery operations have caused the displacement of aboriginal peoples, the death of workers, and environmental damage, negative impacts that the industry has slowly confronted at the prompting of unions, local

communities, environmentalists, and citizen groups. Some of the
people profiled below have played a part in that change.

RANDOLPH W. DIAMOND

Diamond was born in Campbellford, Ontario, February 26, 1891, and
as he grew up he dreamed of being a doctor. However, a year working
at a refinery in Toronto between high school and university changed
his mind, and he graduated from the University of Toronto in 1913
with a degree in mining and metallurgy. After working for a mining
company in Montana, Diamond accepted a job with the Consoli-
dated Mining and Smelting Company of Canada Ltd. (now known as
Cominco) in Trail, B.C.

From 1917–20, Diamond led a five-man team in the development
of a radical new process for ore separation known as differential froth
flotation. It was the first successful large-scale differential flotation
operation, and today the process is a standard method of ore recovery. It helped Cominco increase production, but in so doing the
company also increased air pollution in the surrounding area.
Diamond came up with the solution of a chemical fertilizer plant to
convert sulphur-dioxide emissions into a useful product. The plant
began production in 1931 as one of the earliest efforts at industrial
pollution control. Diamond retired from Cominco in 1956 with many
awards to his credit. He died in 1978.

JAMES GORDON

Gordon was born May 26, 1898, in Glenvale, Ontario, near Kingston.
He graduated from Queen's University in 1920 with a degree in chemistry, and then worked as a researcher studying the complex ores
in the Cobalt, Ontario, area. In 1929, he joined the newly formed
Ontario Research Foundation as assistant director, and while there
analyzed nickel-bronze, iron ores, the use of ammonia gas, and other
mining processes.

In 1936, Gordon was hired by Inco to direct process research at its new laboratory at Copper Cliff, Ontario. He and his research team developed the matte flotation method of copper–nickel separation, replacing the fifty-year-old Orford method. This proved to be the first major improvement in nickel metallurgy since the Orford process was devised, and it greatly reduced the discarding of minerals that were difficult to recover. The laboratory also developed other mining processes, each of which increased the ability of Inco to capture precious metals contained in ore deposits.

In 1948, Gordon was awarded the Medal of the Canadian Institute of Mining and Metallurgy, and in 1957 he was awarded the James Douglas Gold Medal by the American Institute of Mining, Metallurgical, and Petroleum Engineers, for his contributions to refining processes. In 1960, he was elected president of both the International Nickel Company of Canada and its subsidiary, the International Nickel Company of New York. Gordon died in 1980.

LLOYD PIDGEON

Lloyd Pidgeon was born in Markham, Ontario, but as he grew up his father, who worked as a minister, moved the family around Canada. Pidgeon studied undergraduate chemistry at the University of Manitoba, and then obtained his master's and Ph.D. from McGill University in 1929. He then worked at Oxford University for several years before joining the National Research Council of Canada.

While there, Pidgeon developed the process for the production of high-quality magnesium metal using the reaction between calcined dolomite and ferrosilicon. Magnesium was not mined at the time because no process existed, and Pidgeon's process remained to be tested. A pilot plant proved successful, and led to the formation of Dominion Magnesium, with Pidgeon as director of research.

Magnesium plants were opened during the Second World War, as the light, strong metal was best for many uses, aircrafts, for example. In 1943, Pidgeon was appointed head of the department of metallurgical engineering at the University of Toronto (U of T), although he continued to consult with Dominion Magnesium. He also contributed to the development of processes for the production of calcium and strontium which helped Canada become a world leader in the production of these two metals.

Among other awards for his achievements, Pidgeon was appointed to the Order of the British Empire in 1946, and to the Order of Canada in July 1996. He retired in 1969 from U of T.

NEIL GEORGE

George was born in 1908 and grew up in Winnipeg. He received a B.Sc. in 1936 from the University of Manitoba, and then went to work for the International Nickel Company of Canada (a predecessor of Inco Ltd.) in Sudbury, Ontario. Among other jobs, George was a miner and a shift foreman, and eventually general safety engineer for Inco.

Throughout his career, George concerned himself with safety issues. He was appointed director of safety for the Western Quebec Mines Accident Prevention Association in 1948, and by 1964 he had cut the accident rate by about 90 per cent at association member mines, the lowest accident rate ever recorded by any similar mining group in the world. George also developed what is now known through the mining world as the Five Point Safety System. He died in 1988.

LOUIS RENZONI

Louis Renzoni was born in the right place for a career in mining, Copper Cliff, Ontario, which became the site of Inco's research mine in 1936. Renzoni's mother took him for a brief visit to Italy when he was seven months old in 1914, but when the war began they were prevented from returning to Canada until 1920. After high school, Renzoni attended Queen's University and obtained a master's in chemical engineering in 1936. He worked briefly at a consulting firm, then joined Inco at its nickel refinery in Port Colborne, Ontario.

Over the next forty years until his retirement, Renzoni's achievements would earn him recognition as the most knowledgeable scientist in the nickel refining business. He was part of a team that developed substitute materials for nickel refining and recovery methods for cobalt in the late 1930s; he developed a process that ended the need to grind, roast, and smelt ore to produce nickel metal anodes; he created a method for separating out the high-sulphur-bearing mineral called pyrrhotite, allowing the company to produce more while at the same time reducing its sulphur dioxide emissions; and he oversaw early changes that reduced sulphur dioxide emissions by at least 35 per cent.

Renzoni died in 1993 well regarded and much awarded for his achievements, from which Inco is still benefitting. With senior executive and then president Robert Stanley at the helm over a fifty-year period (he also developed earlier improvements to refining processes), and with Renzoni's refining improvement discoveries, Inco went on to become the world's leading producer of primary nickel, a position it still holds with 27 per cent of the world market.

FRANKLIN SPRAGINS

Franklin Spragins was born in Natchez, Mississippi, in 1914 and grew up in Texas. He obtained his electrical engineering degree from Rice University there in 1938, and after a few jobs moved to Canada in 1942 to join Imperial Oil. He did exploration work for the company in Saskatchewan, Alberta, and the Northwest Territories for a few years, and in 1949 he was made manager of a new division to explore oil sands development. In 1965, Syncrude Canada was founded to further establish the development efforts, and Spragins was its first president.

In his role, Spragins stressed the need to develop alternative sources to the western oil fields, predicting that they would be depleted over the years. He recognized that oil sand development needed new technology to be successful because oil sand is very abrasive and sticky. Under his leadership, Syncrude became the world leader in oil sands technology, mining technology, research and development, and operations, a position it still holds today. Spragins died in 1978.

WALTER CURLOOK

Born in 1929 in Coniston, Ontario, Curlook began part-time work at Inco's metallurgical plants in Sudbury when he was only fifteen. He obtained a Ph.D. at the University of Toronto and then returned to Inco. Throughout his career, Curlook has registered twelve mining-process patents for such areas as developing a process to roast pelletized nickel sulphide, improvements to the carbonyl process, bulk mining methods such as vertical crater retreat mining (which doubled productivity), and in automation and the adaptation of computer and laser technology.

Curlook also directed Inco's sulphur dioxide emission abatement program at Sudbury. This $600-million program, completed in 1993, is likely the largest environmental project ever completed by the mining industry. Curlook has received many awards, including an appointment to the Order of Canada in 1996.

CLAUDE COACHE, DENNIS JACOB, AND
FABIEN MILLER OF NORANDA

Coache, Jacob, and Miller, researchers at the Noranda Technology Centre, developed the Cavity Monitoring System (CMS), an underground measurement device now used in many mines throughout the world. The system has been patented in the U.S and Canada and produced by Optech, an Ontario-based manufacturer that helped build the prototype, since 1993.

The CMS automatically measures up to 53,000 points of the inside dimensions of an underground mine cavity with a laser beam in less than an hour, and then creates a three-dimensional image of the cavity on a computer. Before the CMS was developed, technicians seeking to measure underground rock cavities risked danger because they needed to enter the potentially hazardous areas. In addition, the CMS has helped decrease the amount of rock brought to the surface because it can pinpoint where valuable ore is located in a cavity.

In the past five years, one hundred CMS units have been sold and millions of dollars saved through more efficient ore-extraction processes by the users. For their invention, the researchers won the 1998 $25,000 Award of Distinction from the Manning Awards Foundation.

Noranda has developed other industry-leading technologies in the past, including its Gaspé Puncher. The Puncher, so named because it was developed at Noranda's Gaspé smelter in the early 1960s, sends steel bars through air pipes of copper and nickel converters and bath smelting reactors. Air injected through the pipes causes the molten metal to freeze in certain points, thereby clogging the pipes.

Before the Puncher was invented, two or three people would manually push the steel bars through the pipes, a demanding and sometimes dangerous job. In addition to ending this hazardous job, the Puncher also had the effect of increasing copper production by 13 per cent in its first year. Now, almost all copper and nickel smelters use the Puncher, for which Noranda won the 1998 Falconbridge Innovation Award from the Canadian Institute of Mining, Metallurgy, and Petroleum (CIM).

POLARIS MINE – WORLD'S MOST NORTHERLY MINE

Cominco Ltd., an international mining and metals company, is the largest zinc concentrate producer in the world and the fourth-largest zinc metal producer. Its zinc operations include the Polaris Mine on Little Cornwallis Island, approximately one hundred kilometres from the magnetic North Pole in the Northwest Territories. The Polaris Mine, which also produces lead concentrate, is the world's most northerly base-metal mine.

Polaris, which employs about 250 people and has been in operation since 1982, is also known for its technological innovations in permafrost mining. The ground that holds the mine is frozen to a depth of five hundred metres, and if it was allowed to thaw the metal ore would deteriorate and the mine would crumble. To prevent this from happening, the mine is cooled by a refrigeration system from June to September.

Crushed ore is moved from the mine site to a refinery by a two-kilometre-long conveyor system. The ore is stored in a storage facility until ships can access the mine during the only (usually) ice-free months of the year, June, July, and August. Approximately 250,000 tonnes of zinc and lead concentrate are shipped from the mine to European smelters annually.

OLIVIA POOLE
INVENTOR OF THE JOLLY JUMPER

Necessity is often the mother of invention, but in this case a mother's seven children provided the need for her creation. In the early 1950s, Olivia Poole moved with her family to British Columbia from the White Earth Reservation in Minnesota, where she had grown up. Living in Vancouver, Poole developed the Jolly Jumper by combining traditional native design and modern technology.

The device is a harness, suspended by a spring attached to the ceiling, which holds a small child slightly off the floor and allows it to jump up and down. A similar harness was used by people on Poole's reservation, but she added the spring and used different material for the harness. By 1959, Poole and her husband were running a factory in North Vancouver that produced thousands of Jolly Jumpers every month.

Since then, millions of children in Canada, the U.S., Britain, and Australia, among other countries, have both strengthened their leg muscles and kept themselves amused by bouncing up and down in Jolly Jumpers. The Pooles have not owned the business for several years.

RON FOXCROFT
INVENTOR OF THE FOX 40 WHISTLE

Whistles, whether used by referees, dog owners, police, or people lost in the woods, are not much use if they jam. Ron Foxcroft, a professional referee from Hamilton, Ontario, had more than enough experience with jammed whistles as he and his colleagues called violations of the rules of the game on fields, courts, and rinks over the years.

The little cork pea in the whistle would jam or freeze too often, causing missplays or embarassment for the referee.

After he missed a call because of a whistle jam in the men's basketball Olympic finals in 1976 in Montreal, Foxcroft, along with his sons Steve and Dave, undertook the challenge of building a better whistle. Unable to find a bank to support their efforts with a loan, they invested $100,000 of their own money and connected with Chuck Shepherd, an Oakville, Ontario, design consultant, to develop the whistle.

By 1987, fifteen prototypes later, they had perfected a new pealess whistle. Foxcroft called it the Fox 40, a combination of his name and his age when he had the whistle patented. Since then, Promold Corporation, a plastics moulding company in Stoney Creek, Ontario, has made the whistle by ultrasonically welding together the two high-impact plastic halves, instead of gluing them, making the whistle even more durable.

The whistle has been adopted for use by the National Football League, the National Basketball Association, the U.S. National Collegiate Athletics Association (NCAA), the Canadian Football League, FIFA (the governing body for soccer), and FINA (the governing body for water polo and swimming). Ron Foxcroft has used the whistle himself at four NCAA men's basketball final tournaments. In addition, the American Red Cross, the U.S. Coast Guard, the U.S. Army, the Royal Life Saving Society of Canada, and the boy and girl scouts associations all use the whistle.

The Fox 40 whistle is sold in over one hundred countries, and was also used at the Olympics in Seoul in 1988 and in Atlanta in 1996.

DUTHIE BOOKS
WORLD'S FIRST ON-LINE BOOKSTORE

In 1977, Celia Duthie was in Egypt and planning to pursue studies at Cambridge University in England. However, her father, Bill, fell ill and so she returned home to Vancouver to stand in for him at the family bookstore. She led the bookstore through expansion to six stores with over 100,000 titles in stock, but in 1999 was forced to file for bankruptcy protection and cut back to one store, citing increased competition from the Chapters bookstore chain as one reason for the restructuring.

In 1985, Duthie installed a computerized inventory system for the stores. It was the first step in a nine-year process that would see Duthie Books Ltd. become the first virtual bookstore in the world. In June 1994, Duthie launched the store's Web site with 50,000 titles that could be viewed, and then ordered by e-mail. The site provoked responses from around the world, and since then has grown to 100,000 titles.

In addition to its global on-line presence, Duthie Books is also connected to the Vancouver community, supporting literary events and projects such as a television series focusing on writers and a program supplying children's books to disadvantaged communities. The success of other on-line bookstores, especially Amazon.com, has overwhelmed Duthie's achievement somewhat; nevertheless, her store remains the first, if not now the foremost, bookstore to have a presence on the Internet.

S P O R T

Canadians have achieved many firsts and foremosts in the world of sport. Some of these world-beating performances were detailed in *Canada Firsts*. While many other Canadians are world-champion sports stars, it would take an entire book to describe all of their achievements. Set out in this chapter are highlights from some of the most notable Canadian athletes in a wide variety of sports.

Percy Williams's double-gold performance at the 1928 Olympics (detailed below) is considered by many to be the greatest achievement of any Canadian in international track and field competition, if not in all international sporting competitions. However, given that many athletes faced barriers to competing in those days because of racism, lack of funding, or lack of participation by their country in the Olympics (barriers which still exist today for some athletes), modern-day participants probably face more truly global competition when they enter a track, court, course, rink, or other field of competition.

Women were excluded from many areas of sporting competition for decades. Discriminatory rules prevailed until very recently in some cases. After the 1928 Olympic games, despite stellar performances by Canada's women athletes (see details below), Canada's representative to the international Olympics association voted against allowing women to compete in the Olympics in the future. At the time, the Pope and many other world leaders felt that strenuous physical activity was physiologically and psychologically unsuitable for women. Although Canada's representative was on the losing side of the 1928 vote, women were excluded from running races longer than 100 metres and participating in many Olympic sports until decades later. For example, a women's 1,500-metre race was not held until the 1972 Olympics.

To give a sense of the growth in international competition that has occurred as barriers to competition have been lowered, consider that at the first modern Summer Olympic Games in 1906 in Athens, Greece, only 311 male athletes from 13 nations participated. At the 1952 Games in Helsinki, Finland, 4,407 athletes from 69 nations participated (518 of them women). Participation has increased enormously since then, especially by women athletes. At the Summer Games in Barcelona, Spain, in 1992, 10,563 athletes from 172 countries participated, including 3,008 women.

While international competition in some non-Olympic sports has not increased at the same rate as in the Olympics, increases have occurred nonetheless in almost all sports. Of course, anyone who becomes first or foremost in the world in a sport, as in any other area of society, is first or foremost of those who attempted the feat. Many people in the world continue to face barriers to participation in sport, as well as in other areas of their life, or simply choose not to participate. For example, athletes with disabilities continue to be excluded from the Olympics and world championships, as detailed below.

Unfortunately, in many sports the use of performance-enhancing drugs has become an additional factor helping some reach the top of the world, while those who stay clean are forced to compete on a supposedly level playing field. While some have been caught using illegal drugs, such as Canada's Ben Johnson, many others likely have not. As a result, for example, it cannot really be determined how much better Canadian Dave Steen could have done in the decathlon at international competitions. Steen, who never took performance-enhancing drugs, won the bronze medal in the decathlon at the 1988 Summer Olympics in Seoul, Korea.

The sporting achievements by Canadians set out in this chapter should be regarded in these various contexts. Hopefully, some day the world will change in ways that will eliminate the need to add qualifiers to these and other firsts and foremosts in the world.

FIRSTS AND FOREMOSTS IN BASEBALL

CANADIANS INVENTED BASEBALL AND BASEBALL GLOVES

Although no one has claimed responsibility for inventing the Canadian version of baseball, and American Abner Doubleday is invariably credited with inventing the game in 1839, a group of Canadians actually played the first game a year earlier. On July 4, 1838, in Beachville, Ontario (near London), the local team gathered to play a neighbouring township's team.

The game they played was an adaptation of the English games of rounders and cricket, which also featured a pitcher, batters running bases, and fielders. The main differences with the game played today were that no gloves were worn, bats were not standard sizes, batters were allowed to wait for a pitch they liked, and an out occurred when the base runner was hit by the ball. In the 1860s, standard rules were adopted by the national association, and hitting the base runner was replaced with tagging for an out. By 1900, baseball was the most popular sport in the country.

Canadians also played key roles in inventing baseball gloves. Art "Foxy" Irwin is given the most credit, although Phil Powers, a catcher with the London, Ontario, Tecumsehs, is also cited as one of the first to experiment with wearing a glove in the late 1870s. Born in Toronto on February 14, 1858, Irwin was raised in Boston and by 1880 was one of the best shortstops in baseball. Three years later he broke two fingers on his left hand trying to catch a hit. So he could keep playing, Irwin bought an oversized glove and stuffed it with padding to protect his fingers. Within a few years, several other players were also using gloves.

CANADIAN BASEBALL PLAYERS – FOREMOST IN THE WORLD

The first ever international baseball game occurred in the 1860s when the Woodstock, Ontario, Young Canadians played the Atlantic Club of Brooklyn, New York, with Woodstock winning 75 to 11 (high scores were common then because batters could wait for the perfect pitch).

In the 1870s, several leagues were created including the five-team Canadian Base Ball Association, and the U.S. National League, and the U.S. International Association. While baseball games attracted large crowds across Canada, international games and games in the U.S. were more professional and widely recognized. In exhibition games in 1876 and 1877, the first years of the Canadian league, the London, Ontario, Tecumsehs defeated the National League champion Chicago White Stockings and the International Association's champion team from Pittsburgh.

Following these early cross-border challenges, several Canadian players were recruited by U.S. teams and had successful careers. For example, Tip O'Neill recorded the highest batting average in history, .492, when he played for the St. Louis team in 1887. Born in Brantford, Ontario, on May 25, 1858, O'Neill played in the outfield for the Woodstock, Ontario, team before he headed south. At that time, walks were counted as hits, but even if you take away his walks, O'Neill's average was still .435 for the season. He also led the league in doubles, triples, and home runs that season. O'Neill died December 31, 1915, but was not inducted into Canada's Sports Hall of Fame until 1994.

Another successful Canadian player was George "Mooney" Gibson from London, Ontario, who set a major league record in 1909 when he caught 133 consecutive games for the Pittsburgh Pirates, 23 more than the previous record. In 1910, Russell Ford of Brandon, Manitoba, used sandpaper to scuff the baseball (legal at the time), helping his curve ball and him to win 26 games as a rookie for the New York Yankees. On June 16, 1926, Jack Graney from St. Thomas, Ontario, became the first player to wear a number on his uniform. And in 1941, Jeff Heath of Fort William, Ontario ended the season with 199 hits, beating the totals of Ted Williams, who hit .408 that year with 185 hits, and Joe DiMaggio, who had hits in 56 consecutive games but only 193 hits in total. All three were selected for the all-star team that year.

In the early 1940s, the Second World War depleted the ranks of U.S. major league baseball. Chicago Cub owner Philip Wrigley came up with the idea of the All-American Girls Professional Baseball League as a way of keeping ballparks busy and fans entertained. However, not all the women who played were American. Fifty-three Canadians played in the league during its existence from 1943 to 1954, and although they represented only 10 per cent of all players, the Canadians made their mark. For example, Gladys Davis of Toronto was the league's first batting champion, hitting .322 for the Rockford Peaches. Olive Bend Little from Moose Jaw set a strikeout record that was unequalled. Nearly one million people watched the league's games in 1948, but the men's league soon overshadowed the women's league and it folded. The story of the league was not recognized by the Baseball Hall of Fame until the mid-1970s, and was told in the 1992 film *A League of Their Own*.

In 1997, Larry Walker of Maple Ridge, B.C., set or tied nine records for Canadian-born major league baseball players on his way to becoming the National League's most valuable player with 22 of 28 first-place votes. Playing for the Colorado Rockies, he had one of the best seasons of any baseball player ever, ending up second in batting average with .366, second in home runs with 49, third in runs-batted-in with 130, second in runs scored, and with 33 stolen bases and a slugging percentage of .720. No one in the National League had ever had as many home runs combined with as high a batting average.

Walker was also only the third player in baseball history to have more than 200 hits, 40 home runs, and 30 stolen bases in a season. And he became only the fifth player in the National League to have a slugging percentage above .700. In addition, his total bases were 405, the first time a major league player had more than 400 since 1978, the ninth-highest total ever in the National League, and the highest total by a National League player since 1948. Of the 405 total bases, 199 were on extra base hits, tying Stan Musial for the major league record.

Walker began his career with the Montreal Expos, and in 1994, when it looked as if they were headed to the World Series, he was hitting .322 with 19 home runs, 44 doubles, and 86 runs-batted-in. However, the baseball strike that year ended his and the team's chances for a championship. In 1995, he began playing with the Rockies. He has been selected for the all-star team four times, including three years in a row from 1997 to 1999.

THE RIDEAU CANAL SKATEWAY
LONGEST IN THE WORLD

The Rideau Canal was built between 1826 and 1832 to link Ottawa through other canals and rivers to Kingston, on Lake Ontario. This route for water travel shortened the trip and avoided the St. Lawrence River, thereby protecting British military forces from attack by their American or French enemies. In the winter, a 7.8-kilometre section of the canal that winds through the centre of Ottawa freezes over and creates the longest skating rink in the world.

Known as the Rideau Canal Skateway, the ice surface has been maintained since 1971 by the National Capital Commission, an agency that controls government-owned land and parks in the Ottawa area. On average, one million people skate on the canal each winter from late December until the spring thaw. Heated shelters, snack bars, skate rental shops, and washrooms dot the canal, and first-aid staff patrol its length daily to ensure safety for skaters.

The Skateway is the focal point of Ottawa's mid-February Winterlude festival that features entertainment and ice- and snow-sculpting competitions.

LOUIS CYR
WORLD'S STRONGEST MAN

Louis Cyr was born on October 10, 1863, as Noe Cyprien in St-Cyprien-de-Napierville, Quebec (then Canada East). He was very large as an infant, but became even more enormous, weighing almost 64 kilograms at age eleven, and 165 kilograms at his peak, with a 152-centimetre chest and 84-centimetre thighs and biceps. When he was fifteen, his family moved to Lowell, Massachusetts, and Louis, as he was now called, began to work as a lumber jack. He won his first strong-man competition there in 1881 at age eighteen when he lifted a Percheron horse.

The following year, Louis returned to Montreal, where he became a police officer. He won the weightlifting championship of North America in 1885 and the world championship in 1892. Both competitions were far less formal or organized than today's meets. However, in all championships and challenges Cyr was undefeated until 1906, when he retired.

That year, he defeated Canada's reigning strong man, David Michaud, in a lifting challenge of several boulders of increasing size and weight. The largest boulder, which only Cyr lifted, turned out to weigh 237 kilograms. In winning the challenge he also won the hand of Melina Comtois.

His list of other feats of strength is more than impressive. In London, England, on January 19, 1889, he lifted in succession 250 kilograms with one finger, 1,869 kilograms on his back, and 124 kilograms above his head with one hand. He returned to Canada with one of the Marquis of Queen Mary's horses after winning a bet that he could hold two driving horses to a standstill, one tied to each arm. And in 1895 in Boston he lifted a platform holding eighteen large men weighing 1,967 kilograms, believed to be the heaviest weight ever lifted by a man.

From 1894 to 1899, Cyr toured with the Ringling Brothers and Barnum and Bailey circuses, challenging local strong men along the way. His final competition was against twenty-nine-year-old Hector

Decarie in 1906. The two men were tied in the competition until the fourty-four-year-old Cyr lifted a 1,302-kilogram platform that Decarie could not budge.

Cyr died at the young age of forty-nine on November 10, 1912, in St-Jean-de-Matha, Quebec, the victim, in part, of his belief that eating up to nine kilograms of meat a day was healthy and gave him his strength. From age thirty-seven on, as a result of his diet, Cyr suffered the kidney ailment Bright's disease.

Another Canadian, Doug Hepburn, inherited Cyr's title as the world's strongest man when he won the 1953 world weightlifting championships. A much more formal competition than Cyr ever participated in, the championships were the high point of Hepburn's career. For his achievement, which involved lifting a total of 471.74 kilograms, Hepburn was selected as Canada's male athlete of the year.

TOM LONGBOAT
ONE OF CANADA'S FOREMOST LONG-DISTANCE RUNNERS

Tom Longboat faced struggles in his life that many other athletes never have to contend with, especially natural athletes like Longboat. Born June 4, 1887, on the Six Nations Reserve near Brantford, Ontario, Longboat (his native Onandaga name was Cogwagee, which means "Everything") spent most of his early life helping his mother on their farm after his father died when he was five. He was forced to learn English at the mission boarding school in his community, and left school at age twelve.

For the next few years he worked on farms around the region, but he also ran periodically. On Victoria Day in 1905, he entered the Caledon Fair eight-kilometre race and placed second. Impressed by his performance, another aboriginal runner, Bill Davis of the Mohawk First Nation, guided Longboat's training over the next year. In 1906, Longboat won the Caledon race by 400 metres. That year he also won the 30.5-kilometre race around Burlington Bay held annually by the city of Hamilton, beating the other runners by three minutes.

In April 1907, Longboat entered and won the Boston Marathon, beating the course record by over five minutes. As a result, he became a national hero in Canada. His stature attracted some not so helpful attention, however, as he entered into a contract with Tom Flanagan and Jim O'Rourke and soon began running for their Irish-Canadian Athletic Club. Rumours persisted throughout the relationship that Flanagan and O'Rourke were betting on his races, and paying Longboat with proceeds, and he almost lost his amateur status as a result.

Longboat almost missed the 1908 Olympics for another reason, as a case of boils prevented him from participating in the Canadian team trials. He was named to the team, but he collapsed in the final leg of the marathon and didn't finish the race. However, he turned professional, and through several subsequent races Longboat backed up the opinions of many people at the time that he was the world's best long-distance runner.

For example, on December 15, 1908, he beat Dorando Pietri, the Olympic gold medallist, in a race at Madison Square Garden in New York, winning $3,000. And on February 5, 1909, he defeated Alfie Shrubb in the professional world-championship race. After the race, Flanagan sold his contract with Longboat to a promoter from the U.S. for $2,000.

When he lost his next race, Longboat learned a hard lesson about the fleet feet of fame, which can carry a career away in the blink of an eye. Always a controversial sports hero because of prevailing negative stereotypes about aboriginal people, the media quickly turned against Longboat, and it did not help when he was charged for drunkenness in 1911. He served with the Canadian Forces in the First World War, and was wounded twice.

When he returned to Canada, Longboat found his spouse had remarried soon after hearing a mistaken news report that he had died in battle. He took odd jobs and ended up working as a garbageman. On June 9, 1949, Longboat died of pneumonia. He was inducted into Canada's Sports Hall of Fame in 1955.

Since Longboat's world-beating runs, other Canadians have gone on to top the world in long-distance running. For example, Edouard Fabre won the Boston Marathon in 1915 and 1927 as well as many other competitions, including a race on snowshoes. John Miles was only eighteen years old when he stunned the field, including the Olympic champion, by winning the 1926 Boston Marathon in a time more than four minutes faster than the course record. In 1929, Miles won the Marathon with an even faster time. And Gerard Cote won the Boston Marathon in 1940, 1942, 1943, and 1948. He could have won in other years as well, and possibly the Olympic gold, but he was overseas serving with the Canadian army during the Second World War (the 1940 and 1944 Olympic Games were cancelled as a result of the war). In all, Cote competed in 264 races, including 75 marathons, and garnered 112 victories.

Jerome Drayton also had a very successful career, winning the Fukuoka Marathon in Japan, home of the unofficial world championship marathon competition, in 1969, 1975, and 1976. In 1970, Drayton set the world record for ten miles, and in 1975 he set the world record for the indoor three-mile race. He also won the Boston Marathon in 1977. All of these runners have been named to Canada's Sports Hall of Fame.

COMMERCIAL GRADUATES BASKETBALL CLUB
WORLD CHAMPIONS

From 1915 to 1940, the Commercial Graduates Basketball Club of McDougall Commercial High School in Edmonton, Alberta, reigned supreme over all other women's basketball teams, playing for the love of the game and not much else. They won 96 per cent of their games, 49 out of 51 domestic titles, were world champions for seventeen consecutive years, and had a winning streak that lasted for 147 consecutive games.

The Grads financed their travel to tournaments around the world through proceeds from ticket sales. They played twenty-three times in the North American-wide Underwood International Championships, sponsored by the Underwood typewriter company, and won every time. In their final tournament in 1940, the tournament trophy was awarded to them as a memento of their incredible winning record.

Because women's basketball was not sanctioned as an Olympic sport until 1976, the Grads never competed for a medal. However, exhibition games were arranged in conjunction with the Olympics in 1924, 1928, 1932, and 1936 and the Grads won every game they played and outshot their opponents 1,863 points to 297.

In three European Tours the Grads won all twenty-four games they played. Their only significant loss came in the first North American Championship series held in 1933, but they returned to win the tournament in 1934, 1935, and 1936.

Coached by Percy Page, forty-eight women played with the Grads through the years, almost all of them the product of a local farm team system that Page developed for junior high-school teams. In 1940, the Canadian Air Force took over the Grads' playing facility as part of the war effort and the team disbanded. By that time the Grads had won 108 local, provincial, western, national, international, and world titles.

ETHEL CATHERWOOD
WORLD-RECORD HIGH JUMPER

Born in 1909 in Haldimand County, Ontario, Ethel Catherwood was raised in Saskatoon, Saskatchewan, and went on to represent the whole country in a world-beating manner. In the summer of 1926, Catherwood suddenly became a top national athlete when she entered the high jump competition at the Saskatoon city championships and equalled the Canadian record of 1.511 metres. On Labour Day that year at a competition in Regina, she became the top athlete when she broke the world record.

As they still do in many cases today, amateur athletes relied on patrons to help them find employment that allowed them time for training and competing. A Toronto millionaire named Teddy Oke quickly decided to add Catherwood to the list of athletes he supported, and so she and her sister moved to Toronto to work in his investment brokerage offices. Oke also hired an experienced coach, Walter Knox, to guide Catherwood's training.

Catherwood was soon dubbed "The Saskatoon Lily" and comments in news stories on her physical beauty were almost more common than reviews of her performance in competitions. As her winning ways continued, and her reputation as a beautiful athlete grew, she even received offers from Hollywood agents.

In July 1928, the Canadian Olympic trials were held in Halifax. Catherwood set a new world record in that competition of 1.6 metres before 5,000 fans. Although her record would remain Canada's best until 1954, it was soon bettered by Carolina Gisolf of Holland.

That summer, Catherwood travelled with the six-member Canadian women's team to Amsterdam, Holland, for the Olympic competition. Everyone on the team did well, including Catherwood, who beat Gisolf and the other competitors to win the gold. With her win, the women's team also won the overall team title. She is the only Canadian woman ever to win an individual gold medal in Olympic track and field competition.

Catherwood returned home to a hero's welcome, but soon married and moved to San Francisco to settle down, never to compete again. Catherwood was inducted into Canada's Sports Hall of Fame in 1955. She died September 26, 1987.

Another Canadian had great success in the Olympic high jump. Duncan McNaughton, born December 7, 1910, competed at the 1932 Games and won the gold with a jump of 1.97 metres.

FIRSTS AND FOREMOSTS IN SHORT-DISTANCE TRACK RACES

Many of the world-record holders in short-distance track races through the past century have been Canadians, and many of them have turned in performances that have stunned the world.

PERCY WILLIAMS – WORLD'S FASTEST MAN IN THE 1920s

Canadians have been the fastest sprinters in the world a few times over the past several decades, recording exciting world championship and Olympic wins with record-setting runs.

Percy Williams was Canada's unlikely first sprinting hero. He had a damaged heart caused by childhood rheumatic fever, and would claim two decades after his career that he didn't like running and was glad to get out of the sport. Despite this, before a leg injury forced him to retire in 1932, Williams would beat the fastest men in the world, many of whom probably loved what they were doing.

Born in Vancouver on May 19, 1908, Williams was small compared to many other runners, and weighed only fifty kilograms when he was eighteen. That year, however, his sprinting impressed Bob Granger, an experienced coach, enough to take on guiding Williams's training for the next few years.

In the spring of 1928, Williams travelled to Hamilton, Ontario, for the Canadian Olympic trials. He surprised everyone by winning the 200- and 100-metre races and tying the 100-metre Olympic record. In another race that year he tied the world record of 9.6 seconds for the 100-yard sprint.

On July 30 in the finals at the Olympics in Amsterdam, Holland, Williams surprised everyone again by winning the 100 metres. Two days later, he also won gold in the 200-metre finals. He returned home a hero, and his hometown presented him with a sports car and $500, among other gifts.

Following his Olympic victories, Williams confirmed his title as fastest sprinter in the world by winning indoor races in New York, Chicago, Boston, and Philadelphia. Over the next two years, he set a world record for the 100 metres of 10.3 seconds (on August 9, 1930), and a world record of 4.9 seconds for the 45-yard sprint. His 100-metre world record would stand until Jesse Owens ran the distance in 10.2 seconds on June 20, 1936. After his racing career, Williams became a businessman in Vancouver. He died November 29, 1982.

Cyril Coaffee's sprinting achievements are also worthy of note, especially since he beat Percy Williams twice and other top sprinters several times in the mid 1920s. Born February 14, 1897, Coaffee tied the world record of 9.6 seconds for the 100-yard dash in 1922 at the Canadian track and field championships. His time was Canada's national record for over twenty-five years, and he also held the national title for the 200-yard race for several years. Coaffee died July 3, 1945. Both Williams and Coaffee have been inducted into Canada's Sports Hall of Fame.

CANADIAN WOMEN'S RELAY TEAM – FASTEST IN THE 1920s

Fanny Rosenfeld, Myrtle Cook, Ethel Smith, and Florence Bell made up Canada's 4 x 100-metre relay team at the 1928 Summer Olympics, the first Olympics at which women were allowed to participate in this and other track and field events.

Rosenfeld, born December 28, 1903, and known as Bobbie, worked in a chocolate factory at the time. Cook, born January 5, 1902, also worked in a factory; Bell was still a high school student; and Smith, born in 1907, was a legal secretary.

At the time of the Games, Cook held the Canadian titles in the 60- and 100-metre races. She had set the 100-metre world record at the Canadian Olympic trials in Halifax earlier that summer. However, Cook was disqualified from the 100-metre Olympic final when she had two false starts. Rosenfeld and Smith were also in the race. Rosenfeld came second in a close finish that many still maintain should have been regarded as a tie (in those days, photo finishes and electronic timing did not exist, so judges were positioned at the finish line to determine finish order). Smith, who was Canada's 220-yard champion at the time, won the bronze medal.

When it came to the relay, however, the four women combined to set a world record in the semi-finals, and then broke it in winning the finals with a time of 48.2 seconds.

Rosenfeld went on to be named Canada's female athlete of the half century (1900–1950) for her achievements on the track and also in hockey and softball. She died November 14, 1969. Along with Cook, who died March 18, 1985, and Smith, who died December 31, 1979, she has been inducted into Canada's Sports Hall of Fame.

MARK MCKOY – 50-METRE HURDLES WORLD-RECORD HOLDER

Another Canadian who had a successful track and field career is Mark McKoy. Born in Jamaica in 1962, McKoy moved with his family to Toronto at a young age and attended high school and York University there. A long-term competitor at the international level in high hurdles, including three appearances in the Olympic finals, McKoy became one of the foremost hurdlers in the world in 1986. On March 5 of that year at a race in Kobe, Japan, McKoy set the world record for indoor 50-metre hurdles with a time of 6.25 seconds.

In 1992, McKoy won the gold medal for the 110-metre hurdles at the Olympics in Barcelona, Spain. McKoy also holds the Canadian record of 7.41 seconds for 60-metre hurdles, set at a race in Toronto, Ontario, on March 13, 1993. At the 1996 Olympics in Atlanta, Georgia, McKoy competed for Austria.

BRUNY SURIN AND DONOVAN BAILEY – WORLD SPRINT RECORD-HOLDERS IN THE MID 1990s

Between Percy Williams and Bruny Surin, whose career is detailed below, Canada has had few world-class male sprinters. One of them, Harry Jerome, tied the 100-metre world record with a time of ten seconds on July 15, 1960. Unfortunately, at the Olympics later that summer he pulled up lame in the final race. However, Jerome went on to win a bronze medal in the event at the 1964 Olympics. Sadly, he died in 1982 at the young age of forty-two of a brain seizure.

Ben Johnson was just out of high school that year, and two years later he won the bronze medal in the 100-metre event at the 1984 Olympics in Los Angeles. Johnson seemed to be having a world-class racing career, but was stripped of his gold medal, and his world record for the 100 metres at the 1988 Olympics, for taking a banned drug.

Born in Au-Cap-Haitien, Haiti, on July 12, 1967, Bruny Surin moved with his family to Montreal, Quebec, in 1975. He began competing in track and field as a long jumper and triple jumper, but switched to sprinting in 1989. Since then, he has come close to some world records while setting others. In his first year, Surin came tenth in the 60 metres at the World Indoor Championships, but he improved quickly and in 1993 won the world championship in the event. On February 13 of that year at a meet in Leivin, France, Surin set the world record for 60 metres with a time of 6.45 seconds.

In 1995, Surin successfully defended his world champion 60-metre title with a time of 6.46 seconds, setting the record for the meet, held in Barcelona, Spain, that year. However, his world record for this distance was beaten in 1998 by American Maurice Greene (who ran 6.39 seconds). Surin's 1993 record time is still a Canadian record.

Donovan Bailey is another Canadian sprinter who has beaten the world a few times in impressive fashion. Born December 16, 1967, in Manchester, Jamaica, Bailey moved to Oakville, Ontario, when he was twelve to live with his father. He studied business administration at Sheridan College there and started a consulting business after graduation. Unlike most other sprinters, Bailey started training and running seriously quite late, when he was twenty-three years old. He had run track in high school, but took a break for several years, although he played basketball at Sheridan.

Despite Bailey's late start, he was soon winning races in Canada, although not at the international level. In 1994, he met coach Dan Pfaff at the world championships, and began training with him at the University of Texas in Austin. Pfaff helped Bailey refine his running style, and he soon began to make his mark. In April 1995, he set the Canadian 100-metre record with a time of 9.99, and then won the world championship that summer in Göteborg, Sweden, with a new personal best of 9.97 seconds.

The next year, Bailey ran even faster. He set the world indoor 50-metre record on February 9 at a meet in Reno, Nevada, with a time of 5.56 seconds. Then, on July 27, 1996, at the Olympics in Atlanta, Bailey won the 100-metre gold medal and set a new world record of 9.84 seconds. Slow out of the blocks compared to a couple of his competitors, Bailey took over the field toward the end of the race. The silver went to Namibia's Frank Fredericks (9.89 seconds) and the bronze to

Ato Boldon of Trinidad and Tobago (9.9 seconds), the fastest times three people have ever recorded in a 100-metre race.

Since then, Bailey has had difficulties maintaining his world-beating 100-metre style. While he still won several races, he lost his world champion title in 1997, coming second with a time of 9.91 to Maurice Greene. In 1998, he also won a few races on the track and field tour, but then in the fall he tore his Achilles tendon playing a game of pick-up basketball, and was not able to return to racing until June 1999.

In February 1999, Maurice Greene tied Bailey's indoor 50-metre world record, and then on June 16 at a meet in Athens, Greece, Greene broke Bailey's 100-metre record with a time of 9.79 seconds.

Bruny Surin also runs the 100 metres; however, he was overshadowed in the event in Canada from the late 1980s to the mid 1990s, first by Ben Johnson, and then by Donovan Bailey. At the 1995 World Championships, for example, Surin came second to Bailey with a time of 10.03 seconds. In the summer of 1998, however, Surin began to shine, beating Bailey to win the Canadian championship with a time of 9.89 seconds. In the 1999 season, Surin ran even faster, ranking near the top of the field in many races and winning the Canadian 100-metre championship in late June with a wind-aided time of 9.88 seconds, the fastest time ever recorded on Canadian soil. Topping that achievement, Surin came second on August 22 in the 100-metre race to Maurice Greene at the World Track and Field Championships in Seville, Spain, with a time of 9.84 seconds, tying Donovan Bailey for the second-fastest time ever recorded for 100 metres. After the race, Surin hinted of greater things to come when he said he had not run a technically perfect race.

Bailey and Surin continue to try to regain the sprinting world records they have held, and to set new records, and they are joined by other younger Canadian sprinters with the same goal.

MEN'S 4 X 100 METRES RELAY TEAM – FOREMOST IN THE WORLD

Donovan Bailey and Bruny Surin have also been part of the Canadian 4 x 100 men's relay team since 1994. That year, along with teammates Robert Esmie and Glenroy Gilbert, they won the gold medal at the Commonwealth Games in Victoria, B.C., setting the Commonwealth record with a time of 38.39 seconds.

Although they have not broken the U.S. team's world record of 37.40 seconds for the race, they won the gold medal at the World Championships in 1995, and Olympic gold at Atlanta in 1996 with their best time to date of 37.69 seconds. Their Olympic win, along with Bailey's 100-metre win, gave Canada its first double-gold performance in track and field since 1928. In 1997, the relay team successfully defended their world-championship title. That year, the relay team was awarded the Jack W. Davies Trophy for outstanding athletes and the Dr. Phil Edwards Memorial Trophy for outstanding track athletes by Athletics Canada.

Unfortunately, last-minute changes to the team led to problems during the early rounds of the race at the 1999 World Championships. The team was disqualified, and will have to wait until the 2000 Summer Olympics in Sydney, Australia, to re-establish their winning ways.

It is also worthy of note that the women's 4 x 100 metre relay team, made up of Angela Bailey, Marita Payne, Angella Taylor, and France Gareau, came second at the 1984 Summer Olympics in Los Angeles with a time of 42.77 seconds. At the same Games, the women's 4 x 400 relay team, made up of Charmaine Crooks, Jillian Richardson, Molly Killingbeck, and Marita Payne, also came second, with a time of three minutes, 21.21 seconds.

MONTREAL CANADIENS
MOST SUCCESSFUL PROFESSIONAL SPORTS TEAM

The Montreal Canadiens have won more championships, division titles, and playoff games than any other professional sports team in the world. Although they have not won the National Hockey League's Stanley Cup since 1993, the Canadiens have won twenty-three overall, including the highest number of consecutive championships ever in the league, five in a row from 1956 to 1960. Along the way, the team has made the most appearances in the championship finals, thirty-two, including a league-leading ten consecutive appearances from 1951 to 1960.

Other years have not been quite as successful, but the Canadiens have still made the playoffs a league-leading sixty-nine times, including twenty-four consecutive seasons from 1971 to 1994. In 1993, the Canadiens also registered the most consecutive playoff victories in a single season when they won eleven straight games.

The Canadiens also share the record with their opponents for the shortest overtime game played in the NHL. On May 18, 1986, Montreal beat the Calgary Flames after only nine seconds of overtime, with a final score of 3–2. On March 24, 1936 (and on into the wee hours of March 25), another Montreal NHL team, the Maroons, played 116 minutes and 30 seconds of overtime against the Detroit Red Wings, finally losing the longest overtime ever played by a score of 1–0.

FIRSTS AND FOREMOSTS IN ICE HOCKEY

As detailed in *Canada Firsts,* the game of ice hockey as it is played today originated in Canada. Canadians have gone on to record many other firsts and foremosts in the game, including winning the men's world championships and world junior championships too many times to mention, and the men's Olympic gold four times straight from 1920–32, and also in 1948 and 1952. These victories, and others in world cups and other tournaments, have not settled the question as to which country is the world's best at ice hockey, mainly because no country's team has an unbeaten record. However, the achievements set out below make it clear that Canadians are leaders of the game in many ways.

HESPELER HOCKEY – OLDEST HOCKEY-STICK
COMPANY IN THE WORLD

Started up in 1908, Hespeler Hockey Inc. is the oldest hockey-stick company in the world. Located in Cambridge, Ontario (the city was created out of the amalgamation of Galt, Preston, and Hespeler in the mid 1970s) the company was owned by Cooper, the sports equipment company, for some time. It was taken over by an independent entrepreneur, and during the early 1990s lack of capital caused the company to decline.

In 1997, First Team Sports of Minneapolis took over Hespeler Hockey at the urging of NHL hockey star Wayne Gretzky. Gretzky was born and grew up in nearby Brantford, and knew the town and company well (see "Wayne Gretzky – The greatest player ever" below). He also invested in Hespeler Hockey, and entered into a contract that year with First Team Sports to develop and promote the company's ice hockey products. In addition to sticks, Hespeler Hockey makes hockey gloves, pants, and elbow and shin pads.

Canada is also home to the world's largest hockey stick and hockey puck. Commissioned and paid for by the Government of Canada for Expo '86 in Vancouver, B.C., the stick and puck are 62.48 metres long and weigh over 28 tonnes. After the summer 1996 world exposition, the stick and puck were floated by barge from Vancouver to Duncan, B.C., and now sit outside the Cowichan Community Centre there.

JACQUES PLANTE – FIRST TO DEVELOP AND
WEAR A GOALIE MASK THROUGH CAREER

Jacques Plante already had a reputation as a superb and innovative hockey player when he stunned his colleagues, opposing players, and spectators by donning a homemade protective face mask during a game in late 1959. Born January 17, 1929, near Mont Carmel, Quebec, Plante was the oldest of eleven children. He began his hockey career playing goal with a factory team in Shawinigan, Quebec, and went on to play junior for the Quebec Citadels before becoming a professional in 1951.

In 1953, Plante was moved up from the farm team Montreal Royals to the Montreal Canadiens for some playoff games. He became the Canadiens' starting goalie for the 1954–55 season. Over the next several years, Plante changed net-minding in many ways, for example, by being the first to stop the puck behind the net and pass it on to a teammate.

At the time, goalies were expected to face the high-speed shots without a mask, although Plante made one to wear at team practices beginning in 1955. By the 1959 season, Plante had scars from 200 stitches on his face, and was fed up. On November 1 that year, in a game against the New York Rangers, a shot by Andy Bathgate hit just below his nose and opened a cut that required seven stitches. A similar shot from Howie Morenz during the 1929–30 season had broken the nose of the old Montreal Maroons' team goalie Clint Benedict, and Benedict wore a mask until he healed.

Benedict was the first to wear a mask in an NHL game, and went on to tend goal for four Stanley Cup-winning teams. Plante followed Benedict's lead that night in 1959 by refusing to return to face the Rangers without his fibreglass mask. Canadiens' coach Toe Blake eventually agreed to allow him to wear it for the rest of the game.

The Canadiens won the game, and the Stanley Cup that season, and Plante wore a mask every game along the way and through the rest of his playing years, the first goalie to do so. He had an amazing career marred only by bouts of asthma which forced him to stay away from smoke-filled rooms, and earned him a reputation as a loner and unreliable player. The reputation was unjustified, however, as Plante helped the teams he played for win several Stanley Cups. He also won the Vezina Trophy as the league's outstanding goalie seven times, and was the first goalie to win the trophy five times in a row.

Plante also refined his goalie mask several times, and set the trend that flourishes today of decorating masks, which are now mandatory equipment for goalies. Plante was traded by the Canadiens to the New York Rangers in 1963, and then left the game from 1965 to 1968. He returned to play with St. Louis (1968–70), Toronto (1970–73), Boston (briefly in 1973), and the then World Hockey Association's Edmonton Oilers (1974–75). He moved to Switzerland in 1975 and lived there until his death in Geneva on February 26, 1986.

BOBBY ORR – ONLY DEFENCEMAN TO LEAD LEAGUE IN SCORING

Bobby Orr completed an amazing feat as a defenceman for the Boston Bruins. Born March 20, 1948, in Parry Sound, Ontario, Orr was the NHL rookie of the year in 1967. In 1970, he stunned the league when his 37 goals and 87 assists made him the league's leading scorer. For his achievement he won the league's Art Ross Trophy, and the Bruins also won the Stanley Cup that season.

In 1975, Orr did it again, winning the Art Ross with 46 goals and 89 assists. During his career, Orr won the Hart Trophy as the NHL's most valuable player three times, and the Norris Trophy for best defenceman eight times. He played with the Boston Bruins from 1966 to 1975 and for the Chicago Blackhawks from 1976 to 1979, when he retired due to knee injuries. In 1979, Orr was inducted into the Hockey Hall of Fame.

WAYNE GRETZKY – THE GREATEST PLAYER EVER

The Great One, as he is known, achieved enough firsts and foremosts in his hockey career to fill a book, including being foremost in most people's minds when they think of the game. Born January 26, 1961, in Brantford, Ontario, Gretzky was already impressive at age twelve, when he scored 378 goals in 68 games playing in his local league. He went on to be named rookie of the year in his first season of Junior B hockey with the Young Nationals in Toronto, and then scored 70 goals and had 112 assists as rookie of the year with the Sault Ste. Marie Greyhounds of the Ontario Hockey League.

In 1977–78, Gretzky was the leading scorer at the world junior hockey championships, and the summer following that season he turned professional, signing a $1 million contract with the World Hockey Association Indianapolis Racers. Within a few months he moved to the WHA Edmonton Oilers and signed a twenty-one-year contract. That season he again won the league's rookie of the year award, scoring 110 points.

The Oilers joined the National Hockey League (NHL) at the beginning of the 1979–80 season, and Gretzky went on to tie Marcel Dionne for the league scoring title with 137 points. He also won the Hart Trophy as the league's most valuable player and the Lady Byng as the league's most gentlemanly player that year. Over the next eighteen seasons, Gretzky won the Hart trophy eight more times, the Lady Byng four more times, the Art Ross Trophy as the league's leading scorer ten times, the Lester Patrick award as the NHL's outstanding player five times, and the Conn Smythe Trophy as the most valuable player in the playoffs twice.

Gretzky holds 62 NHL scoring records, the most of any player, including: most goals in a season, most points in a season, most assists in a season, most goals in a career, and most times winning the scoring title (including seven times in a row). During his NHL career he played with the Edmonton Oilers, the Los Angeles Kings, the St. Louis Blues, and the New York Rangers, and with those teams made the playoffs sixteen times, winning the Stanley Cup four times with the Oilers.

Gretzky was selected by the Associated Press as the top male athlete of the 1980s. And in January 1998, he was voted the greatest hockey player ever by a panel of fifty experts put together by the respected sport magazine *The Hockey News*. He also won the Lou Marsh Award as the Canadian male athlete of the year four times.

In spring 1999, Gretzky retired from professional hockey. His final game on Sunday, April 18, 1999, in which the Rangers played the Pittsburgh Penguins before a sell-out crowd, was watched by the largest audience ever to view a *Hockey Night in Canada* broadcast, with an average audience of 2.162 million people and a peak audience of

2.811 million. Just over two months later, the league announced that it was going to waive the standard three-year waiting period and induct Gretzky into the Hockey Hall of Fame in a ceremony on November 22, 1999.

After Gretzky's retirement, controversial studies claimed that Canadian Mario Lemieux was the best point-scoring forward of all time. This claim raised the point that in many sports, and many other parts of society, it is often difficult to determine who is first or foremost. Researchers at the Texas A&M University placed Lemieux above Gretzky based on an analysis of scorers from 1948 on that attempted to equalize various factors in the different eras of the game.

The researchers estimated that if Gretzky and Lemieux were playing at their peak at the same time, Lemieux would have outscored Gretzky by six points over a season. However, the researchers also concluded that Gretzky was the most accomplished player, in terms of overall achievements in his career, in any sport.

Other commentators responded to the claims about scoring prowess by pointing out that, if statistics before 1948 were included in the study, other players such as Newsy Lalonde would have a much better rate of goals scored per game played than either Lemieux or Gretzky. And, of course, others pointed to Gordie Howe's stellar career records, including winning six Hart Trophies, six Art Ross Trophies, one Lester Patrick trophy and four Stanley Cup-winning teams. In addition Howe, born March 31, 1928, was named a first team all-star twelve times.

MANON RHÉAUME – FIRST WOMAN TO
PLAY PROFESSIONAL HOCKEY

Manon Rheaume started playing hockey when she was five years old. Born February 24, 1972, in Lac Beauport, Quebec, Rheaume grew up to be a skilled goalie. However, she had to overcome many barriers to play the game she loved, and still struggles with a societal bias against women playing hockey. Having proven herself in many games, she secured a spot on the Trois Rivières Draveurs team of the Quebec

Major Junior Hockey League. Her first game in net for the team was on November 26, 1991, in a game against the Granby Bisons.

The next season, on September 23, 1992, Rheaume tended goal for one period for the Tampa Bay Lightning in a National Hockey League (NHL) exhibition game against the St. Louis Blues. She stopped seven of nine shots on goal. Afterwards, she was signed to a three-year contract with the farm team, the Atlanta Knights. Her first game as a professional player came December 13 of that year against the Salt Lake City Golden Eagles.

Rheaume continued playing professionally with various farm teams from 1993 to 1997. In addition, she played for the Canadian Women's Hockey Team at the World Championships in Finland in 1992. The team won all three games she played in, and the gold medal, and she recorded two shutouts and was named tournament MVP. In 1994 at the World Championships in Lake Placid, New York, the team again won the three games Rheaume played in and the gold medal. Rheaume was also named to the All-Tournament team.

Rheaume was also the goalie for the Canadian Women's Olympic Hockey team in the first official women's tournament in Olympic play. In 1995, 1996, and 1998 she played roller hockey in Canada and the U.S. in the Roller Hockey International League.

CANADIAN WOMEN'S HOCKEY TEAM – FOREMOST WOMEN'S TEAM
Several other Canadian women, and women around the world, have overcome many of the same hurdles as Manon Rheaume to play hockey. Changing alone, eating alone, and bunking alone as they work their way up through various leagues, all women eventually face a hurdle yet to be overcome, playing hockey for a living as a professional. There is no professional women's league and, despite Rheaume's accomplishments, not likely to be room in the men's league for women players in the future.

As a result, when the women on Canada's national team finish playing a tournament, they have only unpaid and local industrial leagues to return to for regular practice and play. Still, returning from international tournaments, Canada's women players have always brought back something they, and the country, can hold up with pride.

In twenty-five games at five consecutive world championships, the Canadian team did not lose one game, bringing home the gold every time. In the most recent final game of the championships, held March 14, 1999, in Espoo, Finland, Canada beat the U.S. team 3–1 to win the title. The only major loss the Canadian team has suffered was at the 1998 Winter Olympics in Nagano, Japan when they lost the gold-medal game against the U.S.

As the game and leagues develop and increase their profile, more girls and women are taking up the sport. There are an estimated 30,000 females playing hockey in Canada, compared to one million males. Many people estimate that after the 2002 Winter Olympics in Salt Lake City, Utah, a women's pro league will form, as by then there will likely be enough players and fans to make it viable.

FIRSTS AND FOREMOSTS IN ALPINE SKIING

As detailed in *Canada Firsts,* Canada's national men's downhill ski team, known as the "Crazy Canucks," won several World Cup races between 1975 and 1984, including Steve Podborski's overall world championship in 1982. While other Canadians have reached the podium in alpine skiing, only Canada's women skiers have won gold. In recognition of their achievements, detailed below, all of these women have been inducted into Canada's Sports Hall of Fame.

LUCILLE WHEELER – WORLD CHAMPION IN
DOWNHILL AND GIANT SLALOM

Born January 14, 1935, Lucille Wheeler began skiing when she was two. At the relatively young age of twelve, she won her first national junior title, and she earned a spot on the national team only two years later.

Wheeler trained hard, including spending five winters in Kitzbuhel, Austria. Her training paid off when she won a bronze medal in the downhill at the 1956 Cortina Winter Olympics, the first-ever Olympic ski medal won by a Canadian. But two years later Wheeler would do even better, stunning the world of skiing that was dominated by European teams when she won both the downhill and giant slalom events at the world championships.

ANNE HEGGTVEIT HAMILTON – OLYMPIC SLALOM GOLD-MEDALLIST AND WORLD CHAMPION

Although she was born in Ottawa, Anne Heggtveit Hamilton's ski career was greatly influenced by her parents' Norwegian heritage. Her parents were from Telemark, Norway, where telemark skiing was invented, and alpine skiing in general had a long history. Only two years after Heggtveit Hamilton appeared in the world on January 11, 1939, her roots began to show when she started skiing.

At age seven, she was already winning competitions, and one year later was inspired by Canadian figure skater Barbara Ann Scott's wins at the world championships and the Olympics (see story in *Canada Firsts*). Only a few years later, Heggtveit Hamilton began her own climb to the top of the world, winning several slalom, giant slalom, and downhill races through the 1950s. For example, in 1954 she became the youngest winner of the Holmenkollen Giant Slalom event in Norway in the fifty-year history of the events.

At the 1960 Olympics in Squaw Valley, U.S., Heggtveit Hamilton became a Canadian hero when she beat U.S. skier Betsy Suite and the rest of the field to win the slalom, the first Canadian skier to win gold. Her margin of victory of 3.3 seconds is the largest ever recorded for that race.

That year, Heggtveit Hamilton also won the overall world slalom and overall world alpine combined titles. Heggtveit Hamilton is a Member of the Order of Canada.

NANCY GREENE – FIRST TO WIN OVERALL AND
GIANT SLALOM TITLES IN SAME SEASON

Nancy Greene only began ski racing seriously when she was fourteen years old. She overcame her relatively late start very quickly, however, becoming a skilled skier. Born May 11, 1943, Greene's determination was also tested by several injuries early in her career.

In 1967, Greene hit her stride, winning three straight World Cup races to take the overall title and the giant slalom title. The next year, she had a magical season. At the Winter Olympics, Greene won the gold medal in the giant slalom and the silver medal in the slalom. She also won nine World Cup races in a row, again winning the women's overall world championship along with the overall giant slalom championship. Greene was the first alpine skier in the world to win these two titles in the same season.

Greene was appointed to the Order of Canada in 1967 and named Canada's female athlete of the year in 1968. She also has a provincial park, a lake, and a street named after her in B.C.

BETSY CLIFFORD – YOUNGEST SKIER EVER TO WIN WORLD
CHAMPIONSHIP

Born October 15, 1953, Betsy Clifford was on the international ski circuit at an age when most young people are just beginning to explore their hometown. When she was only fourteen, she became the youngest Canadian skier ever to compete in the Olympics. Although she didn't win a medal, her races at the 1968 games in Mexico provided her with valuable experience.

In 1970, Clifford again set a record, becoming the youngest skier ever to win the world championship, held in Val Gardena, Italy, that year.

Although she couldn't repeat her feat, Clifford came close in subsequent years, winning the silver medal in the World Cup slalom in 1971, and coming second at the world downhill championship in 1974. She retired in 1976 at the relatively young age of twenty-three.

OTHER WORLD-BEATING CANADIAN WOMEN ALPINE SKIERS

In contrast to Betsy Clifford, Gerry Sorensen was twenty-one years old before she skied a season with Canada's national ski team. Born October 5, 1968, Sorensen hadn't started skiing until she was ten years old, and as a result many people felt she was too old to develop further when she joined the national team, and therefore had little chance of success at the international level.

However, Sorensen's career became an example of the adage "better late than never." In 1981, she won a World Cup downhill race at Haus, Austria, the first victory in ten years by a Canadian woman. And the next year she won the World Alpine Downhill Championship, only the second Canadian woman ever to achieve this feat. Not surprisingly, Sorensen was voted Canada's most outstanding female athlete of the year for 1982.

Born May 4, 1957, Kathy Kreiner was only twelve when she won her first major race, becoming the youngest skier ever to win the Mont Tremblant-Tashereau downhill. Five years later, Kreiner broke through at the international level, winning the World Cup giant slalom race at Pfronten, Germany. Two years later, in 1976, she captured the gold medal in the giant slalom event in her second Olympic competition. That year, Kreiner was named Canada's outstanding female athlete of the year.

Kerrin Lee-Gartner was born September 21, 1966, in Trail, B.C., and grew up in Rossland, B.C. Nancy Greene was a close neighbour in the town, and provided inspiration to Lee-Gartner's alpine skiing dreams. Those dreams came true in 1988 when Lee-Gartner won the gold medal in the downhill race in Meribel, France, at the Albertville Winter Olympics. Her victory was the first time a Canadian skier, male or female, topped the world in the Olympic downhill event.

Born February 13, 1969, in North Bay, Ontario, Kate Pace Lindsay started skiing when she was five. In 1987, she was selected for Canada's national team, and spent the next ten years on the team becoming one of the best skiers in Canadian history.

Before retiring at the end of the 1998 season, Pace Lindsay finished on the World Cup medal podium six times, won three Canadian downhill championships, and competed in the Olympics twice. Her foremost moment came in 1993 when she won the world downhill championship race despite competing with a broken wrist. In recognition of her accomplishment, she was named Canada's female athlete of the year for 1993.

PATRICK MORROW
FIRST PERSON TO SCALE THE HIGHEST PEAKS ON EVERY CONTINENT

Patrick Morrow was born in the mountainous area of Invermere, B.C., on October 18, 1952, the year before Sir Edmund Hillary and Tenzing Norgay reached the summit of Mount Everest. Morrow may have absorbed some of the worldwide excitement about Hillary and Norgay's achievement as an infant, but he clearly went on to inspire others with his own climbing feats.

As he grew up, Morrow developed a wide range of mountaineering skills, eventually becoming a professional climber, mountaineer guide, photographer, and backcountry skier. His career took off when he scaled Mount Everest in 1982. He put all of his skills to the test in completing mountaineering's "grand slam." Over several years, Morrow climbed the highest peaks on the world's seven continents, in North America, South America, Asia, Europe, Africa, Antarctica and Australasia. He became the first person in the world to do so when he reached the summit of the Carstensz Pyramid in Irian Jaya on May 7, 1986.

U.S. businessman Dick Bass claimed that he had completed the grand slam first, however he climbed Australia's Mt. Kosciusko as one of his targets, ignoring Australasia in his series of climbs. Morrow's scaling of the Carstensz Pyramid, a peak nearly twice as high as Mt. Kosciusko, is considered a more accurate and worthy feat as part of the grand slam. In recognition of his feats and contributions to the country, Morrow was appointed to the Order of Canada in 1988.

Along with his spouse, Baiba, Morrow has taken the photos for and written the text of three books, including a chronicle of his seven-summit quest. They have also contributed to many other books, and have won eight national magazine photo awards. Morrow also worked as the publicity stills photographer for the recent Hollywood movies *K2*, and *Seven Years in Tibet.*

The Morrows' home base is now in Canmore, Alberta, and from there they maintain a somewhat hectic schedule of photography workshops, guiding, filming for television networks and the Canadian International Development Agency (CIDA), climbing and travelling.

FOREMOST ATHLETES WITH DISABILITIES

Organized sport for athletes with disabilities has existed for over a century. The sports were initially organized for rehabilitation purposes, as opposed to competition. For example, wheelchair sports were first introduced in 1944 in England as a form of treatment and rehabilitation for people with spinal-cord injuries. Within four years, however, the first international competitions were held, and in 1960 in Rome, the first Olympic-style games for athletes in wheelchairs were held. Canada began to develop its own wheelchair sports program in 1947.

At the 1976 games in Toronto, the idea of merging different disability groups for international sport competition was born. That year, the first winter games took place in Sweden. The Paralympics, as they have come to be known, are now sport events for elite athletes from six different disability groups. The International Paralympic Committee (IPC) coordinates the games, along with world championships. Founded in 1989 out of an earlier, similar organization, the IPC is run by 160 national Paralympic committees and five disability-specific international sports federations.

The Paralympics has grown enormously, from 400 athletes in Rome in 1960 to 3,195 in Atlanta in 1996. More athletes will participate in the Sydney 2000 Summer Paralympics than participated in the 1972 Olympics in Munich. The Paralympics have always been held in the same year as the Olympic Games, and since the 1988 Seoul summer games and the 1992 Albertville winter games they have been held at the same locations.

Events are arranged so that athletes with comparable disabilities compete against each other. Among other categories, wheelchair track-and-field sports are divided into different divisions for paraplegics and quadriplegics, four for track (T1 to T4) and eight (F1 to F8) for field events. For swimming events, freestyle, backstroke, and butterfly are divided into ten classes (S1 to S10) and breaststroke into nine classes (SB1 to SB9). Swimmers are placed in different classes based on a bench press test, a technical test and observation during competition to determine how well they perform in water. For athletes with seeing disabilities, there are three classes based generally on ability to see, from total blindness (B1) to a visual field of five degrees to twenty degrees (B3).

There are eighteen Summer Paralympic event areas, including track and field, basketball, and swimming, and five Winter Paralympic sports include ice sledge racing, and alpine and cross-country skiing. Hearing impaired people do not participate in the IPC competitions, as their own world federation, founded in 1922, continues to organize their own international games called the Silent Games.

An ongoing debate within these sports organizations concerns whether the international events should emphasize participation or competition (which would lead to fewer categories and more overall winners). Another related issue is the integration of athletes with disabilities into the Olympics and world championships.

In 1997 in Canada, responsibility for wheelchair track-and-field sports was transferred to Athletics Canada as part of a process to have a national sports system that serves all athletes equally, but at the international level such integration is just beginning. At the 1996 Olympics in Atlanta, the men's 1,500-metre and women's 800-metre wheelchair races were included as demonstration sports for the fourth time. The events were also included in the 1997 world championships, but athletes who won medals did not receive the tens of thousands of dollars in cash awards that able-bodied athletes receive.

As some commentators have pointed out, using a wheelchair in a race is no different than using a bicycle, and so both sports (among others) should be included in the Olympics. However, with 271 events already in the Summer Olympics, the International Olympic Committee has been reluctant to expand the games, and has instead considered removing some current events.

As in other sports, many of Canada's athletes with disabilities have reached the top of the world in their events; indeed, so many that space does not allow a description of all of their achievements (the Canadian team at the 1996 Paralympics included twenty-four world-record holders and eighteen world champions). Stories of a few of the past and current standout performers appear below.

ANDRÉ VIGER AND CLAYTON GERAIN – FOREMOST IN LONG-DISTANCE WHEELCHAIR RACES

Born September 27, 1952, in Windsor, Ontario, André Viger moved with his family to Quebec when he was one year old. In 1973, as a result of a car accident, Viger became a paraplegic. He began to train himself on a wheelchair two years later, and in 1979 began to compete seriously, completing his first marathon that year.

In 1984, 1986, and 1987, Viger won the Boston Marathon in the men's wheelchair category (men were first allowed to participate in 1977, while the women's wheelchair race was first held in 1975). Viger also won the marathon at Oita, Japan, every year from 1984 to 1987. Although Viger does not currently hold any world records, he held the marathon record from 1986 to 1988, has held records in the past in track and field, and still holds six Canadian records.

In 1992, at age forty, Viger won the 10,000-metre gold at the Summer Paralympics in Barcelona, Spain. The 1996 games in Atlanta, Georgia, were Viger's fifth Paralympics. In recognition of his achievements, Viger was appointed to the Order of Canada in 1989.

Clayton Gerain, of Regina, Saskatchewan, broke through on the

international level in 1992, setting the world records in the T2 1,500-
and 5,000-metre races that year (as of January 1999 he still held these
records). At the 1996 Paralympics in Atlanta, Gerain won the gold
medal in the 5,000 metres and placed second (to Brent McMahon of
Toronto) in the 1,500 metres and the marathon.

CHANTAL PETITCLERC – FOREMOST FEMALE
SPRINTER IN WHEELCHAIR EVENTS

Born January 15, 1969, in Ste-Foy, Quebec, Chantal Petitclerc is the
daughter of a construction contractor and a librarian. When she
was thirteen years old, a barn door fell on her and she lost the use
of her legs.

Petitclerc has been on the national team since 1989, competing in
wheelchair track events. She came third in the T4 200 metres and 800
metres at the 1992 Summer Paralympics, and has improved consistently since then. At the 1994 IPC world championships, Petitclerc
won gold in the 200-metre and 400-metre races.

In 1996, she won two gold and three silver medals at the Summer
Paralympics. Petitclerc has held the world record since 1997 in the T4
100 metres with a time of 16.68 seconds. On July 7, 1999, Petitclerc
recorded her second world record (still to be officially confirmed)
when she won the T4 800 metres event in 1 minute 50.62 seconds at a
competition in Atlanta, Georgia.

Petitclerc also holds the Canadian records for the women's T4 200
metres, 400 metres, 800 metres, 1,500 metres, and marathon. She lives
in Montreal and hosts Lotto Quebec's televised weekly draws.

ANDRÉ BEAUDOIN, JEFF ADAMS, AND DEAN BERGERON –
FOREMOST MALE SPRINTERS IN WHEELCHAIR EVENTS

André Beaudoin of Montreal holds three world records for quadriplegics in the 100-metre, 200-metre, and 800-metre wheelchair
events. Beaudoin began to rise to the top of the world at the 1996
Paralympics, where he won silver in the 100 metres. At the 1998 world

championships in Birmingham, England, Beaudoin won gold in the T2 100-metre, 200-metre, and 400-metre races. He set his three world records winning the events at a competition in Atlanta, Georgia, in July 1998.

Jeff Adams, born November 15, 1970, in Brampton, Ontario, is one of the rare full-time athletes with disabilities. He qualified in 1992 to compete in the 1,500-metre wheelchair Olympic demonstration race; however, his four years of training were thwarted when the push ring on his rear right wheel fell off with 300 metres to go in the race. Adams won a silver in the 800 metres at the Paralympic Games that year, and was part of the 4 x 400-metre relay team that also won silver.

In June 1995, Adams set the world record for the T4 400 metres at a competition in Toronto, Ontario. That year, he won the 1,500-metre demonstration race at the IAAF world championships, improving on his silver medal in the event at the 1994 IPC World Championships. At the 1996 Paralympics, Adams won gold in the 800 metres and silver in the 400 metres. In addition to his world record (which he still held as of January 1999), Adams also holds Canadian records in four other events.

Dean Bergeron of Quebec City is another Canadian wheelchair racer who has had international success. A former NHL prospect when he played for the Shawinigan Cataractes of the Quebec Major Junior Hockey League, Bergeron first broke through in 1994, when he won the gold in the 800- and 1,500-metre races and in the marathon, silver in the 200- and 400-metre events, and bronze in the 100 metres. Since then, Bergeron has won gold in the 200-, 400-, and 1,500-metre races at the 1995 world championships, and gold in the 200 metres at the 1996 Paralympics. Bergeron set the world record for the T2 400-metre event at a competition in Toronto, Ontario, in June 1995 (as of January 1999, he still held the record).

FOREMOST SWIMMERS

Marie Claire Ross was born November 21, 1975, in Kingston, Ontario. In 1992, she joined the national team for disabled swimmers. Ross has a seeing disability, and competes in the B3 category. She has set several world records and won several medals at international competitions.

At the 1992 Summer Paralympics, Ross showed signs of things to come when she won one silver and three bronze medals. At the 1994 IPC World Championships, Ross broke through to win gold in the 100-metre breaststroke, and two years later she won gold again and set the world record for the event at the Paralympics.

Ross also holds the world records for 50- and 200-metre breaststroke, 100- and 200-metre breaststroke on a short course, and the 200-metre individual medley. She lives and trains in London, Ontario.

Other female swimmers to have reached the top of the world include Joanne Mucz, who won triple gold at the 1992 Paralympics and holds three world records in the S9 category, and Elisabeth Walker, who joined the team in 1993 and holds the world record in the S7 50- and 100-metre butterfly events, along with the 100-metre backstroke record.

Michael Edgson, who no longer competes, shone for Canada in the pool from the mid 1980s to early 1990s. He set four long-course and two short-course world records in the B3 seeing-impaired category, records which still stand, while winning gold at the 1992 Summer Paralympics in Barcelona, Spain, and at other competitions.

Andrew Haley, born in Moncton, New Brunswick, has competed for the national team since 1991 while living and training in Ottawa, Ontario. Haley competes in the S9 category, and in 1994 he began to shine by winning three bronze medals at the IPC World Championships. Since then, he has gone on to set world records in the 100- and 400-metre (short course) freestyle races, the 100-metre (short course) and 200-metre (short and long course) backstroke events, and the 200-metre individual medley. Haley also won gold and set the world record for the 100-metre butterfly at the 1998 IPC World Championships.

Walter Wu, of Richmond, B.C., is another male swimmer who has been on top of the world since he joined the national team in 1993. Competing in the B3 category, Wu won four gold medals and set a world record for the 200-metre individual medley race at the 1994 IPC World Championships. Since then, he has set several other world records for the category, including the 400-metre freestyle and the 100-metre backstroke events. He set those records while winning six gold medals at the 1996 Paralympics.

JAY COCHRANE
WORLD'S FOREMOST WIREWALKER

Born May 1, 1944, at more or less sea level in Saint John, New Brunswick, Jay Cochrane would go on to walk high above water across a long wire, the highest and longest combined walk ever. In so doing, Cochrane would set one of his many world records for wire-walking.

At age fourteen, Cochrane ran away from home and joined the Royal Hanneford Circus in Toronto, Ontario. His job was cleaning animal cages, but over the years he was trained as a wirewalker by Mrs. "Struppi" Hanneford, alias Princess Tajana, a well-known aerialist. In 1965, a tower collapsed during his performance with the circus in Toronto, and Cochrane fell more than twenty-seven metres onto a concrete floor. He was severely injured, and his doctors predicted that he would walk with two canes for the rest of his life.

However, Cochrane recovered fully, and during his recovery earned a master's degree in structural engineering at the University of Toronto. His fall had not changed his mind about what he wanted to do with his life, and he was soon back to wirewalking and using his engineering degree to design the rigging for his walks.

In late 1970, Cochrane made his first wirewalk at an extreme height when he walked between the fifty-storey-high Hudson's Bay Towers in his hometown of Toronto, Ontario (he now lives in Florida and New York City). He would repeat the feat in 1973 and 1977.

In 1972, Cochrane set a world record for the farthest distance on a wire when he walked 4.02 kilometres in total by going back and forth forty-one times along a 91.44-metre-long wire strung 36.57 metres above the ground between the Hockey Hall of Fame and the Canadian National Grandstand at the Canadian National Exposition in Toronto. It took Cochrane four hours and thirty-four minutes to complete the feat. And in 1976, Cochrane spent twenty days living on a wire, breaking his world record in 1981 by spending twenty-one days above the ground in San Juan, Puerto Rico. He repeated this feat at Kennywood Park amusement fair in Pennsylvania in 1983.

Cochrane considers his greatest feat to be his walk across the Qutang Gorge, China. In September 1995, he travelled to the nearby city of Fengjie to supervise as the wire was strung across the gorge. As the date of the walk neared, he was visited at his hotel by hundreds of children seeking autographs.

It was the first walk Cochrane ever had to talk himself into doing, and with good reason. The wire was strung 488.65 metres above the Yangtze River and 765.07 metres across the Gorge. On October 28, Cochrane took fifty-three minutes to cross the wire and set the world record for the combined highest and longest wirewalk ever. Cochrane's feat was watched by 200,000 spectators and by 200 million Chinese on television, and commemorated in China with images on stamps, envelopes, watches, and long-distance phone cards.

His walk was also watched closely by the Western media, as the feat was used by the Chinese government to promote its highly controversial Three Gorges Dam project. When completed, the 2.1-kilometre, 185.93-metre-high dam will be the largest in the world and will fill the Qutang Gorge and two other gorges halfway up with water, creating a 400-mile-long lake. Many environmentalists consider the project the most destructive infrastructure project in the world, as it will flood 1,000 cities, including Fengjie, and acres of arable land, and force 1.9 million people to move their homes.

In addition, the dam is being built on unstable land, and if it collapses it could endanger the lives of ten million people. While the World Bank refused to provide funds for the project, export credit agencies from several countries, including Canada (but not the U.S.), have helped finance the over $60 billion cost of the project. Cochrane took a similar stance toward the project as Canada's Export Development Corporation, stating that other countries had no right to question China's plans.

Since crossing the Gorge, Cochrane has continued to create new wirewalking challenges. In 1996, he set the world record for the longest and highest nighttime building-to-building skywalk when he crossed a wire strung 160 metres high and 182.88 metres across between two skyscrapers. His feat was the showpiece of a tourism festival in Shanghai, China, and was watched by 250,000 people.

On November 12, 1998, Cochrane set another world record when he walked blindfolded between the towers of the Flamingo Hilton hotel in Las Vegas, Nevada, on a wire strung 91.44 metres above the ground. His walk was broadcast on the *Guinness World Records: Primetime* television show.

On October 6, 1999, Cochrane began an attempt to break his world record for time spent on a wire in Chong Qing, China. His feat was part of the celebration of the fiftieth anniversary of the People's Republic of China, and he planned to spend twenty-two days on the wire, descending on October 28, the anniversary of his walk across the Qutang Gorge.

In the past, Cochrane has also wirewalked over the famous arch in St. Louis, Missouri, above the Space Ship Earth exhibit at Disney's Epcot Centre (more than three hundred times), across the Minnesota State Fair in St. Paul (three times) and across Silver Springs in Florida, and from the top of the Sports Coliseum to the Space Needle in Hershey, Pennsylvania. In addition, he has wirewalked across more than fifteen stadiums in the U.S. In the future, among many other places, Cochrane would like to wirewalk across Niagara Falls. Charles Blondin completed this feat first in 1859, and the last person to do it was in 1897. Since then, such feats at the Falls have been banned.

SELECTED BIBLIOGRAPHY

Bohnert, Beth. *Canadian Women: Risktakers and Changemakers.* Thornhill: The Women Inventors Project, 1993.

Boulton, Marsha. *Just a Minute: Glimpses of our Great Canadian Heritage.* Toronto: Little, Brown and Company (Canada) Ltd., 1994.

———. *Just Another Minute: More Glimpses of our Great Canadian Heritage.* Toronto: Little, Brown and Company (Canada) Ltd., 1997.

Ellis, Frank H. *Canada's Flying Heritage.* Toronto: University of Toronto Press, 1968.

Farrar, F. S. RCMP. *Arctic Assignment: The Story of the St. Roch.* Toronto: Macmillan of Canada, 1974.

Kearney, Mark, and Randy Ray. *The Great Canadian Trivia Book.* Toronto: Hounslow Press, 1996.

———. *The Great Canadian Trivia Book 2.* Toronto: Hounslow Press, 1998.

Mayer, Roy. *Inventing Canada: One Hundred Years of Innovation.* Vancouver: Raincoast Books, 1997.

Muir, Allen and Dorin, in collaboration with Victor Nymark. *Building the Château Montebello.* Gardenvale, Quebec: Muir Publishing Company Ltd., 1980.

Panabaker, Janet. *Inventing Women: Profiles of Women Inventors.* Thornhill: The Women Inventors Project, 1991.

Are you concerned about democratic reform,
government and corporate accountability
in Canada ?

If so, you can help by supporting

emocracy Watch
émocratie en surveillance

Democracy Watch is one of the foremost citizen
advocacy groups in Canada, and among other
victories, led the campaigns to stop the bank mergers, for
stronger government ethics rules, and for
disclosure of the activities of corporate lobbyists.
Headed up by *More Canada Firsts* author
Duff Conacher, Democracy Watch needs your
support in order to be effective.

Yes, I want to contribute to democratic reform and
corporate accountability in Canada:

Here's my donation of $_____ to Democracy Watch.

☐ My cheque is enclosed *OR* I'd like to contribute by:

Address (if different from address on cheque, or if paying by credit card):	VISA ☐ Mastercard ☐
Name_____	Card number: _____
	Expiry Date: _____ / _____
Address _____	Signature: _____
_____	Please send this form to:
_____	P.O. Box 821, Stn. B, Ottawa, Canada K1P 5P9
	Thank you for your support!